Atomic Dinettes
Mid-Century Kitchen Elegance

Donna S. Baker, Editor

Schiffer Publishing Ltd

4880 Lower Valley Road, Atglen, PA 19310 USA

Published by Schiffer Publishing Ltd.
4880 Lower Valley Road
Atglen, PA 19310
Phone: (610) 593-1777; Fax: (610) 593-2002
E-mail: Info@schifferbooks.com

For the largest selection of fine reference books on this and related subjects, please visit our web site at
www.schifferbooks.com
We are always looking for people to write books on new and related subjects. If you have an idea for
a book please contact us at the above address.

This book may be purchased from the publisher.
Include $3.95 for shipping.
Please try your bookstore first.
You may write for a free catalog.

In Europe, Schiffer books are distributed by
Bushwood Books
6 Marksbury Ave.
Kew Gardens
Surrey TW9 4JF England
Phone: 44 (0) 20 8392-8585; Fax: 44 (0) 20 8392-9876
E-mail: info@bushwoodbooks.co.uk
Free postage in the U.K., Europe; air mail at cost.

The values shown in this book represent a guideline only and are intended to provide readers with a general idea of what they might expect to pay for each piece in today's market. The values shown reflect these items in excellent, near-mint condition, i.e., no pitting on the chrome, upholstery in excellent condition, laminate in excellent condition, etc. Popular retro colors and mid-century modern styling can add to the value. Larger sets may also be valued higher. It is entirely possible to purchase an item for a higher or lower amount than the value shown here, as many factors affect the actual price paid. These factors include condition, scarcity, the venue of the market, and the buyer's relative desire to own a particular item.

Objects depicted in this book may be covered by various trademarks, copyrights, and logotypes. Their use herein is for identification purposes only. All rights are reserved by their respective owners. Lloyd is a registered trademark of Lloyd®/Flanders Inc. This book is not sponsored, endorsed, or otherwise affiliated with Lloyd®/Flanders Inc. or any other companies whose products are represented herein. This book is derived from independent research.

Copyright © 2005 by Levi Heywood Memorial Library Association
Library of Congress Control Number: 2005931968

Designed by Mark David Bowyer
Type set in Van Dijk / Souvenir Lt BT

ISBN: 0-7643-2280-X
Printed in China
1 2 3 4

Acknowledgments

This book would not have been possible without the assistance of the Levi Heywood Memorial Library, 55 West Lynde St., Gardner, Massachusetts 01440. We extend deepest thanks to Director Gail Landy and Local History Cataloger Pam Meitzler for providing access to their wonderful collection of Heywood-Wakefield catalogs and other historical materials. We are also grateful to Travis Smith, Good Eye Mid Century Modern (www.goodeyeonline.com), for providing the furniture values included in this book.

Contents

Foreword 4

Preface 5

1950s Dinettes 6

1960s Dinettes 15

1970s Dinettes 97

Wrought Iron Dinettes 149

Foreword

Although located at a distance from Menominee, Michigan where Lloyd products were manufactured, the public library in Gardner, Massachusetts is fortunate to hold many catalogs of the Lloyd Manufacturing Company, by virtue of the fact that the enterprise was owned for many years by Gardner's furniture giant, the Heywood-Wakefield Company. To have the Lloyd catalogs reproduced here for mid-century modern collectors and enthusiasts to devour is a great privilege—and a fun time capsule. Enjoy!

—Pamela Meitzler
Local History Cataloger
Levi Heywood Memorial Library
Gardner, Massachusetts

Preface

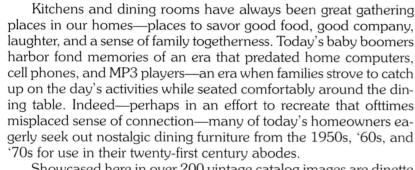

Kitchens and dining rooms have always been great gathering places in our homes—places to savor good food, good company, laughter, and a sense of family togetherness. Today's baby boomers harbor fond memories of an era that predated home computers, cell phones, and MP3 players—an era when families strove to catch up on the day's activities while seated comfortably around the dining table. Indeed—perhaps in an effort to recreate that ofttimes misplaced sense of connection—many of today's homeowners eagerly seek out nostalgic dining furniture from the 1950s, '60s, and '70s for use in their twenty-first century abodes.

Showcased here in over 200 vintage catalog images are dinette sets representing a virtual kaleidoscope of colors and styles from the mid-twentieth century. These inviting and alluring atomic age furnishings start off with classic 1950s chrome and vinyl combinations; move forward to the '60s with comfy Early American designs, molded fiberglass chairs in turquoise and coral, and luxurious high back seating coupled with faux marble tables; then proceed into the shag-carpeted '70s with earthy Mediterranean and other international styles, rich woodgrain tabletops, and even a set of smoke colored acrylic bucket chairs. All were produced by the Lloyd Manufacturing Company, a Michigan based firm established by Marshall B. Lloyd (1858-1927) in 1906. Originally known for its extensive production of wicker furniture, baby carriages, and doll buggies, Lloyd Manufacturing was acquired in 1921 by the more well-known Heywood-Wakefield Company, of Gardner, Massachusetts. Over the next several decades, the company's focus turned from wicker and woven furniture to primarily metal offerings, including metal dinette sets, casual and outdoor furniture, and contract furniture. Lloyd remained a subsidiary of Heywood-Wakefield until that company closed its doors in the late 1970s.

Reproduced here through the generous cooperation of the Levi Heywood Memorial Library in Gardner, Massachusetts, the catalog images comprising this book feature an eye-catching array of tables and chairs from each of the decades represented. An additional section at the end of the book provides a fun look at wrought iron sets that, while produced in the 1960s and 1970s, could easily add a touch of elegance to contemporary kitchens, patios, or all-season rooms.

Note that model numbers and descriptions accompanying each picture were transcribed from original Lloyd catalog copy—slight variations in format and detail therefore reflect the years spanned by this material. Dates shown in parentheses were added for purposes of this book and represent the date of the catalog from which each image was taken, *not* actual production dates.

Dining in style will never go out of style, so pull up a chair, grab a cup of coffee, and relax with this unique reference for vintage furniture collectors, designers, and all who love the retro look of the mid-century years.

1950s Dinettes

Table T-2011 – "Trimline," Sable Finish (1954)
30" x 40" x 48" plastic laminate top with black metal banding. 29 ½"
high. Removable leaf. Steel extension slides. ¾" tubular steel legs. Floor
glides of non-marring clear plastic. Also available in Chrome finish.

Chair C-1010 – "Trimline," Sable Finish (1954)
15 ½" x 15 ½" pad seat. Flared pad back. ¾" tubular steel legs and back
posts. Floor glides of non-marring clear plastic. Overall height
31 ½". Also available in Chrome finish.

Set: $250-350

Table T-2012 – "Trimline," Sable Finish (1954)
30" x 40" x 48" plastic laminate top with self-plastic edge. 29 ½" high. Removable
leaf. Steel extension slides. ¾" tubular steel legs. Floor glides of non-marring clear
plastic. Also available in Chrome finish (T-2018, see next picture).

Chair C-1010 – "Trimline," Sable Finish (1954)
15 ½" x 15 ½" pad seat. Flared pad back. ¾" tubular steel legs and back posts.
Floor glides of non-marring clear plastic. Overall height 31 ½". Also available in
Chrome finish.

Set: $250-350

Table T-2018 – "Trimline," Chrome Finish (1954)
30" x 40" x 48" plastic laminate top with self-plastic edge. 29 ½" high. Removable leaf.
Steel extension slides. ¾" tubular steel legs. Floor glides of non-marring clear plastic. Also
available in Sable finish (T-2012, see previous picture).

Chair C-1018 – "Trimline," Chrome Finish (1954)
15 ½" x 15 ½" thick tapered pad seat. Wing-shaped pad back. ¾" tubular steel legs and
back posts. Overall height 32". Floor glides of non-marring clear plastic. Also available in
Sable finish (C-1011, see page 9).

Set: $300-400

Table T-2013 – "Trimline," Sable Finish (1954)
36" x 48" x 60" plastic laminate top with self-plastic edge. 29 ½" high. Removable leaf.
Steel extension slides. ¾" tubular steel legs. Floor glides of non-marring clear plastic. Also
available in Chrome finish (T-2019, see page 8).

Chair C-1012 – "Trimline," Sable Finish (1954)
15 ½" x 15 ½" box seat with white welt and glass-fibre cushioning. Thick padded back
with handle and concealed posts. Floor glides of non-marring clear plastic. Overall height
32", exclusive of handle. Also available in Chrome finish.

Set: $250-350

Table T-2019 – "Trimline," Chrome finish (1954)
36" x 48" x 60" plastic laminate top with self-plastic edge. 29 ½" high. Removable leaf. Steel extension slides. ¾" tubular steel legs. Floor glides of non-marring clear plastic. Also available in Sable finish (T-2013, see page 7).

Chair C-1020 – "Trimline," Chrome finish (1954)
16 ½" x 16 ½" box seat with white welt and glass-fibre cushioning. Back rods finished black to contrast with chrome frame. 5/8" tubular steel legs and back frame. Floor glides of non-marring clear plastic. Overall height 31 ½". Also available with Sable finish on legs and back frame, chrome finish on back rods; or Sable finish on legs, back frame and back rods.

Set: $250-350

Table T-2010 – "Trimline" Drop Leaf, Sable Finish (1954)
30" x 22" top surface of plastic laminate with black metal banding. Extends to 30" x 47" with two tapered drop leaves in raised position. 29 ½" high. 1" tubular steel legs. Floor glides of non-marring clear plastic. Also available in Chrome finish.

Chair C-1010 – "Trimline," Sable Finish (1954)
15 ½" x 15 ½" pad seat. Flared pad back. ¾" tubular steel legs and back posts. Floor glides of non-marring clear plastic. Overall height 31 ½". Also available in Chrome finish.

Set: $200-300

Table T-2020 – "Trimline," Sable Finish (1954)
42" diameter round top extends to 42" x 54" with removable leaf in place. Surface of plastic laminate with black metal banding around edge. 29 ½" high. Steel extension slides. ¾" tubular steel legs. Floor glides of non-marring clear plastic. Also available in Chrome finish (T-2021, see next picture).

Chair C-1011 – "Trimline," Sable Finish (1954)
15 ½" x 15 ½" thick tapered pad seat. Wing-shaped pad back. ¾" tubular steel legs and back posts. Floor glides of non-marring clear plastic. Overall height 32". Also available in Chrome finish (C-1018, see page 7).

Set: $250-350

Table T-2021 – "Trimline," Chrome Finish (1954)
42" diameter round top extends to 42" x 54" with removable leaf in place. Surface of plastic laminate with black metal banding around edge. 29 ½" high. Steel extension slides. ¾" tubular steel legs. Floor glides of non-marring clear plastic. Also available in Sable finish (T-2020, see previous picture).

Chair C-1020 – "Trimline," Chrome Finish (1954)
16 ½" x 16 ½" box seat with white welt and glass-fibre cushioning. Back rods finished black to contrast with chrome frame. 5/8" tubular steel legs and back frame. Floor glides of non-marring clear plastic. Overall height 31 ½". Also available with Sable finish on legs and back frame, chrome finish on back rods; or Sable finish on legs, back frame and back rods.

Set: $250-350

9

Table T-3008 – Chrome Finish (1954)
30" x 40" x 48" plastic laminate top with stainless steel banding and chrome-plated skirt. 29 ½" high. Removable leaf, wood extension slides. 1" tubular steel legs, chrome-plated. Floor glides of non-marring clear plastic.

Chair C-1029 – Chrome Finish (1954)
15 ½" x 15 ½" thick pad seat cushion. Rectangular pad back cushion. 1" tubular steel legs, chrome-plated. Floor glides of non-marring clear plastic. Overall height 31".

Set: $300-400

Table T-3009 – Chrome Finish (1954)
30" x 50" x 60" plastic laminate top with stainless steel banding and chrome-plated skirt. 29 ½" high. Removable leaf. Steel extension slides. 1" tubular steel legs, chrome-plated. Floor guides of non-marring clear plastic.

Chair C-1030 – Chrome Finish (1954)
15 ½" x 15 ½" thick pad seat cushion. Padded back has decorative contrasting panel. 1" tubular steel legs, chrome-plated. Floor glides of non-marring clear plastic. Overall height 31".

Set: $350-450

Table T-3009 – Chrome Finish (1954)
30" x 50" x 60" plastic laminate top with stainless steel banding and chrome-plated skirt. 29 ½"
high. Removable leaf. Steel extension slides. 1" tubular steel legs, chrome-plated. Floor glides of
non-marring clear plastic.

Chair C-1032 – Chrome Finish (1954)
15 ½" x 15 ½" thick pad seat cushion. Concealed back post, no-mar type back with convenient
handle. 1" tubular steel legs, chrome-plated. Floor glides of non-marring clear plastic. Overall height
33", including handle.

Set: $300-400

Table T-3010 – Chrome Finish (1954)
36" x 50" x 60" plastic laminate top with stainless steel banding and chrome-
plated skirt. 29 ½" high. Removable leaf. Steel extension slides. 1" tubular steel
legs, chrome-plated. Floor glides of non-marring clear plastic.

Chair C-1033 – Chrome Finish (1954)
15 ½" x 15 ½" box cushion seat with molded shredded sponge rubber cushioning and white welt. Thick octagon shaped, no-mar type back cushion with
convenient handle. 1" tubular steel legs, chrome-plated. Floor glides of non-
marring clear plastic. Overall height 33 ¾" including handle.

Set: $300-400

Table T-3012 – Chrome Finish (1954)
36" x 54" x 72" plastic laminate top with stainless steel banding and chrome-plated skirt. 29 ½" high. Self-storing folding leaf with steel extension slides. 1" tubular steel legs, chrome-plated. Floor glides of non-marring clear plastic. Also available with removable leaf.

Chair C-1035 – Chrome Finish (1954)
15 ½" x 15 ½" extra thick cushion with molded shredded foam rubber cushioning and decorative white welt. Extra wide no-mar type shaped back with diagonal contrasting panel, nail-head trim and handle. 1" tubular steel legs, chrome-plated. Floor glides of non-marring clear plastic. Overall height 35".

Set: $400-500

Table T-281 – Chrome Finish (1954)
42" x 60" x 90" plastic laminate top with stainless steel banding around edge and chrome-plated skirt. Two 15" self-storing folding leaves, wood extension slides. Center leg support. 29 ½" high. 1" tubular steel legs, chrome-plated. Floor glides of non-marring clear plastic.

Chair C-117 – Chrome Finish (1954)
15 ½" x 15 ½" pad seat cushion. Tapered pad back. 1" tubular steel legs, chrome-plated. Floor glides of non-marring clear plastic. Overall height 32 ½".

Set: $500-600

Table T-5004 (1954)
30" x 43" x 54" plastic laminate top surface in "Platinum" wood-grained pattern. Self-storing folding leaf, steel extension slides. 29 ½" high. Legs of solid hardwood, finished to match top. Plated steel floor glides. Also available with removable leaf.

Chair C-4004 (1954)
16 ½" x 16 ½" pad cushion seat. Wing-shaped pad cushion back. Solid hardwood legs, in "Platinum" finish. Plated steel floor glides. Plastic or soft fabric covers. Overall height 32 ½".

Set: $500-700

Table T-5004 (1954)
30" x 43" x 54" plastic laminate top surface in "Platinum" wood-grained pattern. Self-storing folding leaf, steel extension slides. 29 ½" high. Legs of solid hardwood, finished to match top. Plated steel floor glides. Also available with removable leaf.

Chair C-4005 (1954)
16 ½" x 16 ½" box seat with glass-fibre cushioning. Curved wing-shaped wood back. Solid hardwood legs, finished in "Platinum." Plated steel floor glides. Plastic or soft fabric covers. Overall height 32 ½".

Set: $500-700

Lloyd

TABLE TOPS
CHAIR COVERS
PATTERNS AND COLORS

BE SURE TO SPECIFY PATTERN AND COLOR WHEN ORDERING

TARTAN

A LLOYD EXCLUSIVE

Tables and Chairs

141 Yellow | 142 Gray | 140 Charcoal | 144 White | 145 Red

← No. 145 Red Tartan for Chair Covers only - not available for Table Tops.

TAFFETA

For

Chairs only

375 Yellow | 378 Brown | 370 Red | 372 Green | 143 Coral

"Taffeta" chair covers have been selected for their ability to tastefully combine with "Tartan" table tops.

TWEED

for

Chairs only

128 Yellow | 127 Ivory | 125 Red | 126 Green | 129 Chartreuse

The tweed chair covers go particularly well with the Platinum table top shown below.

MOTHER-OF-PEARL

For Tables and Chairs

151 Yellow | 150 Gray | 153 Red | 152 Green | Platinum—Table Top only

No. 153 Red Mother-of-Pearl for Chair Covers only - not available for Table Tops.

Chair cover and tabletop patterns, 1954.

1960s Dinettes

Table T-8463 –
Goldtone Finish
(1961)
Chair C-5450 –
Goldtone Finish
(1961)

Set: $500-600

T-8463 TABLE—*Goldtone Finish*
Top: 48" diameter, self-edge, octagon shape.
Base: 3" tubular metal pedestal column with goldtone
  finish. Tapered tubular legs with metal ferrules and
  self-aligning glides.

T-8462 TABLE
42" diameter top, otherwise exactly same as above.
Available in White Velvet and Tawny Walnut only.

Page 2

C-5450 CHAIRS—*Goldtone Finish*
Seat: 16¾" x 15¾" thickly padded box seat, with
  poly foam cushioning and extruded plastic welt.
Back: High, padded, no-mar back rest with back
  posts and top rail welded with smart mitred corners.
  Decorative ornamental grill at top of back of heavy-
  guage metal rod, finished goldtone.
Frame: ⅞" tubular legs and back frame, with metal
  ferrules and self-aligning glides.
Overall Height: 33"

T-8450 "Colonial House" TABLE—*Metallic Bronze Finish*
Top: 42" x 42" x 60" (42" round)—18" leaf.
  Plastic self-edge.
Legs: 1¾" tapered tubular, designed to complement
  "Provincial" styling. Metal ferrules and
  self-aligning glides.
Note: Plastic top in "Maple" only, as illustrated.

C-5455 CHAIR—*Metallic Bronze Finish*
Seat: 18½" x 16¾", with polyfoam cushioning.
  "Provincial" flounce and double welt
  of extruded plastic.
Back: Deep radius, thickly padded oval shaped back rest.
Frame: 1" tubular with tapered legs,
  joints torch-welded. Metal ferrules and
  self-aligning glides.
Overall Height: 31"

Table T-8450 – "Colonial House," Metallic Bronze Finish (1961)
Chair C-5455 – Metallic Bronze Finish (1961)

Set: $350-450

T-8461 TABLE—*Goldtone Finish*
Top: 36″ x 48″ x 60″—12″ leaf. Self-edge, and 3″ matching plastic skirt with anodized gold aluminum bead trim on lower edge.
Legs: 1¾″ tapered tubular with special squared shape top to fit outside of corners of skirt. Metal ferrules and self-aligning glides.

C-5451 CHAIRS—*Goldtone Finish*
Seat: 18½″ x 16½″ box seat is extra wide, has poly foam cushioning and extruded plastic welt.
Back: Smart, thickly padded oval shaped back rest with extruded plastic welt. Decorative gold colored metal ornament suspended between back posts.
Frame: 1¼″ tapered tubular legs and back posts, all joints torch-welded. Metal ferrules and self-aligning glides.
Overall Height: 35½″

C-5452 ARM CHAIR—*Goldtone Finish*
Same as C-5451 except has 19½″ x 17½″ seat and shaped wood arm rests on ⅞″ tubular arms.

Table T-8461 – Goldtone Finish (1961)
Chair C-5451 – Goldtone Finish (1961)
Arm Chair C-5452 – Goldtone Finish (1961)

Set: $600-800

T-8468 TABLE—*Goldtone Finish*
*Top: 42" x 42" x 60" (42" round)—18" leaf. Plastic
self-edge with anodized, gold-colored, extruded
aluminum bead trim.*
*Legs: 1¾" double-tapered tubular, with metal ferrules
and self-aligning glides.*

C-5440 CHAIRS—*Goldtone Finish*
*Seat: Extra wide 20" x 15¼" thickly padded,
oval-shaped box seat with extruded plastic welt.*
*Back: Deep radius, narrow oval-shaped back with
extruded plastic welt. Metal rod decoration.*
*Frame: 1" tapered tubular legs, ⅞" tapered tubular
back posts. Metal ferrules and self-aligning glides.
Wall-saver design.*
Overall Height: 31½"

Page

Table T-8468 – Goldtone Finish (1961)
Chair C-5440 – Goldtone Finish (1961)

Set: $400-500

18

T-8433 TABLE—*Goldtone Finish*
*Top: 36" x 48" x 60"—12" leaf. Anodized,
 gold-colored, extruded aluminum edge banding.
Legs: 1¾" tapered tubular, with metal ferrules
 and self-aligning glides.
Leaf Hanger: For self-storing of extension leaf.*

C-5448 CHAIR—*Goldtone Finish*
*Seat: 16" x 15½" thickly padded "pajama" style box seat
 with extruded plastic welt.
Back: High, contoured, padded no-mar back rest framed in
 capped back posts and cross rail.
Frame: ⅞" tubular legs and back posts, with ⅝" cross
 rail on back. Metal ferrules and self-aligning glides.
Overall Height: 33½"*

Table T-8433 – Goldtone Finish (1961)
Chair C-5448 – Goldtone Finish (1961)

Set: $300-400

T-8466 TABLE—*Goldtone Finish*

Top: 36″ x 48″ x 72″—two 12″ leaves. Plastic
   self-edge with anodized, gold-colored, extruded
   aluminum bead trim.
Legs: 1¾″ double-tapered tubular, with
   metal ferrules and self-aligning glides.

C-5453 CHAIRS—*Goldtone Finish*

Seat: 15¾″ x 15¾″, thickly padded, double welt
   of extruded plastic.
Back: Full height, thickly padded back rest,
   distinctively shaped and set in back frame.
   Double welt.
Frame: ⅞″ tubular with metal ferrules and
   self-aligning glides.
Overall Height: 34″

Table T-8466 – Goldtone Finish (1961)
Chair C-5453 – Goldtone Finish (1961)

Set: $350-450

T-8465 TABLE—*Goldtone Finish*

Top: 36" x 48" x 60"—12" leaf. Plastic self-edge
  with anodized, gold-colored, extruded aluminum bead trim.
Legs: 1¾" double-tapered tubular, with metal ferrules
  and self-aligning glides.
Leaf Hanger: For self-storing of extension leaf.

T-8464 TABLE

Top: 30" x 40" x 48"
  (Otherwise same as above.)

C-5444 CHAIRS—*Goldtone Finish*

Seat: 16" x 16½" thickly padded.
Back: Fully-upholstered, smartly tapered "roll-top"
  design. No-mar construction.
Frame: Legs 1" tapered tubular, fitted with metal
  ferrules and self-aligning glides. Wall-saver
  design. All members of frame have torch-welded joints.
Overall Height: 35"

Page 8

Table T-8465 – Goldtone Finish (1961)
Chair C-5444 – Goldtone Finish (1961)

Set: $350-450

T-8433 TABLE—*Goldtone Finish*
Top: 36″ x 48″ 60″—12″ leaf. Anodized,
   gold-colored, extruded aluminum edge banding.
Legs: 1¾″ tapered tubular, with metal
   ferrules and self-aligning glides.
Leaf Hanger: For self-storing of extension leaf.

C-5443 CHAIRS—*Goldtone Finish*
Seat: 17½″ x 16½″ thickly padded, tapered box seat with
   extruded plastic welt.
Back: Smartly shaped padded back rest offset from
   back posts with metal rods. Extruded plastic welt.
Frame: 1″ tapered tubular legs and back posts.
   ¾″ tubular seat supports. Sturdy, torch-welded
   joints. Wall-saver design.
Overall Height: 34½″

Page 9

Table T-8433 – Goldtone Finish (1961)
Chair C-5443 – Goldtone Finish (1961)

Set: $400-500

22

T-8439 TABLE—*Goldtone Finish*

Top: 36 x 36 x 60 (36" round)—two 12" leaves.
Anodized, gold-colored, extruded aluminum edge banding.
Legs: 1¾" tapered tubular, with metal ferrules and self-aligning glides.

C-5434 CHAIR—*Goldtone Finish*

Seat: 17" x 16" thickly padded box seat, with extruded plastic welt.
Back: Form-fitting decorative wire grill.
Frame: 1" tapered tubular legs, with ¾" back frame.
Metal ferrules and self-aligning glides. Wall-saver design.
Overall Height: 32".

Table T-8439 – Goldtone Finish (1961)
Chair C-5434 – Goldtone Finish (1961)

Set: $250-350

T-8467 TABLE—*Goldtone Finish*
Top: 42" x 48" x 72"—two 12" leaves. Plastic self-edge
with anodized, gold-colored, extruded aluminum bead trim.
Legs: 1¾" double-tapered tubular, with metal ferrules
and self-aligning glides.

C-5439 CHAIRS—*Goldtone Finish*
Seat: 16½" x 16" thickly padded box seat with extruded
plastic welt.
Back: Decorative insert on shaped back.
Frame: ⅞" tubular, with metal ferrules and self-
aligning glides. Wall-saver design.
Overall Height: 32¼"

Page 11

Table T-8467 – Goldtone Finish (1961)
Chair C-5439 – Goldtone Finish (1961)

Set: $350-450

24

T-8432 TABLE—*Goldtone Finish*
Top: 30″ x 40″ x 48″—8″ leaf. Anodized, gold-colored, extruded aluminum edge banding.
Legs: 1¾″ tapered tubular, with metal ferrules and self-aligning glides.
Leaf Hanger: For self-storing of extension leaf.

C-5445-R CHAIRS—*Goldtone Finish*
Seat: 16½″ x 16″ saddle shape of exclusive, solid, molded plastic. Colors cannot fade—White, Cocoa or Natural.
Back: Shaped back of same material as seat.
Frame: 1″ tubular, with self-aligning metal glides. Wall-saver design.
Overall Height: 32″

Page 12

Table T-8432 – Goldtone Finish (1961)
Chair C-5445-R – Goldtone Finish (1961)

Set: $250-350

25

T-8434 TABLE—*Goldtone Finish*

Top: 36 x 48 x 72—two 12″ leaves. Anodized, gold-colored, extruded
    aluminum edge banding.
Leg: 1¾″ tapered tubular, with metal ferrules and self-aligning glides.

C-5430 CHAIR—*Goldtone Finish*

Seat: 16″ x 16″, thickly padded "Pajama" style. Extruded plastic welt.
Back: Thick, deep radius, shaped no-mar back, 17½″ x 10″.
    Extruded plastic welt.
Frame: 1″ tapered tubular with metal ferrules and self-aligning glides.
    Wall-saver design.
Overall Height: 31¾″.

Table T-8434 – Goldtone Finish (1961)
Chair C-5430 – Goldtone Finish (1961)

Set: $400-500

Table T-8431 – Goldtone
Finish (1961)
Chair C-5428 – Goldtone
Finish (1961)

Set: $150-250

T-8431 TABLE—*Goldtone Finish*

Top: 24 x 36—non-extension, with anodized gold-colored, extruded
 aluminum edge banding.
Legs: 1¼″ tapered tubular, with metal ferrules and self-aligning glides.

C-5428 CHAIR—*Goldtone Finish*

Seat: 15½″ x 16″, thickly padded.
Back: Thickly padded and shaped no-mar back. Extruded plastic welt.
Frame: ⅞″ tubular, wall-saver design. Metal ferrules and clear plastic floor glides.
Overall Height: 31″.

T-8456 TABLE—*Goldtone Finish*

Top: 42 x 60 x 96—two 18" leaves. Plastic self-edge with anodized, gold-colored, extruded aluminum bead trim.

Legs: 1¾" tapered tubular, with metal ferrules and self-aligning glides. Extra center-leg support.

C-5429 CHAIR—*Goldtone Finish*

Seat: 16 x 16" thickly padded box seat, with extruded plastic welt.

Back: Heavily padded and shaped no-mar back with extruded plastic welt. Metal rod decoration.

Frame: ⅞" tubular, with metal ferrules and self-aligning glides. Wall-saver design.

Overall Height: 32"

T-3072 TABLE—*Chrome Finish* ▶

Same as T-8456 except has polished, extruded aluminum edge banding.

C-1618 CHAIR—*Chrome Finish* ▶

(Otherwise same as C-5429)

Page 15

Table T-8456 – Goldtone Finish (1961)
Table T-3072 – Chrome Finish (1961)

Chair C-5429 – Goldtone Finish (1961)
Chair C-1618 – Chrome Finish (1961)

Set: $600-800

Table T-8448 –
Extension Drop Leaf,
Goldtone Finish (1961)
Chair C-5429 –
Goldtone Finish (1961)

Set: $150-250

C-5429 CHAIR—*Goldtone Finish*

Seat: 16″ x 16″ thickly padded box seat, with extruded plastic welt.

Back: Heavily padded and shaped, no-mar with extruded plastic welt.
  Metal rod decoration.

Frame: ⅞″ tubular, with metal ferrules and self-aligning glides.
  Wall-saver design.

Overall Height: 32″.

T-8448 EXTENSION DROP-LEAF TABLE—*Goldtone Finish.*

Top: 42″ x 25″ x 84″ (42″ x 25″ closed)—18″ extension leaf. Plastic self-edge.
  Handy pull-out lever extends leg-assemblies.
Legs: 1¾″ tapered tubular, with metal ferrules and self-aligning glides.
  Note: Plastic top available only in Champagne Walnut, Tawny Walnut,
    White Mahogany, Blond Cherry or Sandstone Walnut.

T-8447 EXTENSION DROP-LEAF TABLE

Top: 36 x 25 x 72 (36 x 25 closed)—12″ extension leaf.
  (Otherwise same as T-8448.)

T-8445 TABLE

Top: 30 x 22 x 48 (30 x 22 closed)—(Otherwise same as T-8448.)

T-8446 TABLE

Top: 36″ x 25″ x 60″ (36″ x 25″ closed)—(Otherwise same as T-8448.)

Table T-8444 –
Drop Leaf, Goldtone
Finish (1961)
Chair C-5447 –
Goldtone Finish
(1961)

Set: $150-250

Page 17

T-8444 DROP-LEAF TABLE—*Goldtone Finish*
Top: 36″ x 25″ x 60″ (36″ x 25″ closed). Anodized, gold-colored,
   extruded aluminum edge banding. Handy pull-out
   lever to extend leg assemblies.
Legs: 1¾″ tapered tubular, with metal ferrules and
   self-aligning glides.

T-8455 TABLE
Top: 36″ x 25″ x 72″ (36″ x 25″ closed)—12″
   extension leaf.
   (Otherwise same as T-8444.)

T-8443 TABLE
Top: 30″ x 22″ x 48″ (30″ x 22″ closed),
   (Otherwise same as T-8444.)

C-5447 CHAIRS—*Goldtone Finish*
Seat: 16″ x 15½″ thickly padded box seat with
   extruded plastic welt.
Back: High, contoured, padded back rest.
Frame: ⅞″ tubular with capped back posts.
   Metal ferrules and self-aligning glides.
Overall Height: 34″

Right:
Table T-3068 –
Chrome Finish (1961)
Chair C-1618 –
Chrome Finish (1961)

Set: $400-500

30

T-3068 TABLE—*Chrome Finish*

Top: 42″ x 48″ x 72″—two 12″ leaves. High polish, extruded aluminum banding.
Legs: 1¾″ tapered tubular, with self-aligning metal glides.

T-3067

Top: 36″ x 48″ x 72″—two 12″ leaves. (Otherwise same as T-3068.)

C-1618 CHAIR—*Chrome Finish*

Seat: 16″ x 16″ thickly padded box seat, with extruded plastic welt.
Back: Heavily padded and shaped no-mar back, with extruded plastic welt. Metal rod decoration.
Frame: 1″ tubular with self-aligning metal glides. Wall-saver design.
Overall Height: 32″

Page 21

31

T-3065 TABLE—*Chrome Finish*

Top: 30 x 40 x 48—8" leaf. High polish, extruded aluminum banding.
Legs: 1¾" tapered tubular, with self-aligning metal glides.
Leaf Hanger: For self-storing of extension leaf.

T-3066 TABLE

Top: 36 x 48 x 60 (12" leaf)—(Otherwise same as above.)

C-1620 CHAIR—*Chrome Finish*

Seat: 17" x 16" thickly padded box seat, with extruded plastic welt.
Back: Form fitting decorative wire grill.
Frame: 1" tapered tubular legs, with ¾" back frame. Metal ferrules and self-aligning glides. Wall-saver design.
Overall Height: 32".

Page 22

Table T-3065 – Chrome Finish (1961)
Chair C-1620 – Chrome Finish (1961)

Set: $250-350

T-3064 TABLE—*Chrome Finish*
Top: 24" x 36"—non-extension. High polish extruded aluminum banding.
Legs: 1¼" tapered tubular, with self-aligning metal floor glides.

C-1617 CHAIRS—*Chrome Finish*
Seat: 15½" x 16", thickly padded, shaped seat.
Back: Heavily padded and shaped no-mar back, with extruded plastic welt.
Frame: 1" tubular, with wall-saver design.
Overall Height: 31"

Page 23

Table T-3064 – Chrome Finish (1961)
Chair C-1617 – Chrome Finish (1961)

Set: $150-250

Table T-3071 – Extension Drop Leaf, Chrome Finish (1961)
Chair C-1619 – Chrome Finish (1961)

Set: $150-250

T-3071 EXTENSION DROP-LEAF TABLE—*Chrome Finish*

Top: 36 x 25 x 72 (36 x 25 closed)—12″ leaf. High polish, extruded aluminum banding. Handy lever to extend leg-assemblies.
Legs: 1¾″ tapered tubular, with self-aligning metal glides.

T-3070 TABLE

Top: 36 x 25 x 60 (36 x 25 closed)—(Otherwise same as T-3071.)

T-3069 TABLE

Top: 30 x 22 x 48 (30 x 22 closed)—(Otherwise same as T-3071.)

C-1619 CHAIR—*Chrome Finish*

Seat: 16″ x 16″ thickly padded "Pajama" style, with extruded plastic welt.
Back: Deep-radius, thickly padded no-mar back, 17½″ x 10″. Extruded plastic welt.
Frame: 1″ tapered tubular legs, with metal ferrules and self-aligning glides. Wall-saver design.
Overall Height: 31¾″.

Table T-8478 – "Plymouth House," Bronze Finish (1963)
Top is 36" x 48" x 60" with 12" extension leaf. Has tapered edge protected with anodized gold colored extruded aluminum. Top shown, Maple.

Chair C-5463 – "Plymouth House," Bronze Finish (1963)
Shaped maple finished hardwood back rail decorated with Early American motif. Legs, 7/8". Cover shown, No. 416 White and Red.

Set: $350-450

Table T-8479 – "Plymouth House," Bronze Finish (1963)
42" round top extends to 42" x 60" oval shape as shown. Table has tapered edge protected with anodized gold color extruded aluminum trim. Top shown, Maple.

Chair C-5464 – "Plymouth House," Bronze Finish (1963)
Maple finished hardwood back rail is decorated with Colonial motif. Legs, 7/8". Cover shown, No. 418 Watermelon Red.

Set: $400-500

Table T-8450 – "Plymouth House," Bronze Finish (1963)
42" round top extends to 42" x 60" oval shape as shown. Table has plastic self-edge. Top shown, Maple.

Chair C-5420 – "Plymouth House," Bronze Finish (1963)
Back is amply padded, has special no-mar feature that's kind to walls. Legs, 1" tapered. Cover shown, No. 421 Brick.

Set: $300-400

Table T-8505 – "Plymouth House," Bronze Finish (1963)
42" round top (non-extension), with tapered edge and anodized gold colored extruded aluminum trim. Top shown, Maple.

Chair C-5477 – "Plymouth House," Bronze Finish (1963)
Chair has graceful maple finished hardwood back rest decorated with Early American motif. Legs, 7/8". Cover shown, No. 432 Red.

Set: $300-400

Table T-8504 –
"Harvest Group," Black Finish (1963)
Top is 36" x 48" with both leaves raised and is trimmed with anodized gold colored extruded aluminum banding. Top shown, Red "Filigree."

Chair C-5478 –
"Harvest Group," Black Finish (1963)
Hardwood backrest decorated with quaint Early American floral motif and gold colored finials. Legs, 7/8" Cover shown, No. 430 White "Zephyr Ceylon."

Bench B-5480 –
"Harvest Group," Black Finish (1963)
Seat is 40 ½" wide, seats two. Legs, 7/8". Cover shown, same as on chair.

Set (table and chairs): $350-450
Bench: $200-250

Table T-8494 – Goldtone Finish (1963)
Top is 42" x 48" x 72", including two 12" extension leaves.
Top shown, Tawny Walnut.

Chair C-5465 – High Back, Goldtone Finish (1963)
The majestic sweep of the back gives this chair a truly
distinctive appearance. Legs, 1" tapered. Overall height, 34
½". Cover shown, No. 378 Champagne.

Set: $350-450

Table T-8477 – Goldtone Finish (1963)
Top is 36" x 48" x 72", including two 12" extension
leaves. Top shown, Champagne Walnut.

Chair C-5473 – High Back, Goldtone Finish (1963)
Back is interestingly shaped and accented with metal
mesh "window." Legs, 7/8". Overall height, 36".

Set: $350-450

Table T-8493 – Goldtone Finish (1963)
Top is 30" x 40" x 48". Top shown, White Mahogany.

Chair C-5472 – High Back, Goldtone Finish (1963)
Distinctive back treatment including wire mesh "window" and contour curved back. Legs, 7/8". Overall height 34". Cover shown, No. 383 Turquoise.

Set: $300-400

Table T-8474 – Goldtone Finish (1963)
Top is 36" x 48" x 50" with a 12" leaf. Top shown, American Provincial Walnut.

Chair C-5462   High Back, Goldtone Finish (1963)
Seat and back are Tawny Walnut finished plywood and have contour shaped padded cushions. Legs, 7/8". Overall height, 34 ½". Cover shown, No. 360 White.

Set: $350-450

Table T-8475, Goldtone Finish (1963)
42" round top extends to 42" x 60" oval shape with 18"
leaf in place. Top shown, White "Brushtone."

Chair C-5434 – Goldtone Finish (1963)
Back has form-fitting decorative metal grill. Legs, 1"
tapered. Overall height, 32". Cover shown, No. 412 Beige.

Set: $200-300

Table T-8496 – Goldtone Finish (1963)
42" round top extends to 42" x 72" oval shape with two 15" leaves
in place, as shown. Top shown, Blond Cherry.

Chair C-5429 – Goldtone Finish (1963)
Heavily padded back with special no-mar feature to protect walls.
Legs, 7/8". Overall height, 32". Cover shown, No. 379 Turquoise.

Set: $500-600

Sturdy center leg provides added support and balance to T-8490 table.

Close-up view of knurled leg design and 1¾″ thick plastic self-edge table top.

Table T-8490 – Goldtone Finish (1963)
Top is 42" x 60" x 96" with two 18" leaves in place, as shown. Table gets an added measure of support from sturdy center leg. Top shown, Tawny Walnut.

Chair C-5467 – High Back, Goldtone Finish (1963)
Legs, 7/8". Overall height, 35". Cover shown, No. 430 White.

Set: $500-650

PAGE 6

41

Table T-8487 – Goldtone Finish (1963)
Top is 36" x 48" x 60" with 12" leaf.

Chair C-5468 – High Back, Goldtone Finish (1963)
Legs, 7/8". Overall height, 35". Cover shown, No. 413 White Dot and Dash.

Set: $200-300

Table T-8489 – Goldtone Finish (1963)
Top is 42" x 48" x 72" with two 12" leaves. Top shown,
Sandstone Walnut.

Chair C-5469 – High Back, Goldtone Finish (1963)
Modern hi-back design. Legs, 7/8". Overall height, 36 ½".
Cover shown, No. 406 White Stripe.

Set: $350-450

Table T-8491 – Goldtone Finish (1963)
42" round top extends to 42" x 60" oval with 18" leaf. Top shown, Medallion Inlay.

Chair C-5470 – High Back, Goldtone Finish (1963)
Ornamental bow on back adds interesting decorative effect. Legs, 7/8". Overall height, 36". Cover shown, No. 431 Tan.

Set: $250-350

Table T-8492 – Goldtone Finish (1963)
42" round extends to 42" x 72" oval with two 15" leaves. Top shown, Blond Cherry.

Chair C-5471 – High Back, Goldtone Finish (1963)
Beautiful shield-shape padded backs set these fine chairs apart immediately. Legs, 7/8". Overall height, 35". Cover shown, No. 363 Turquoise.

Set: $400-600

Table T-8497 – Pedestal Base,
Goldtone Finish (1963)
42" round (non-extension) top with
1 ¾" plastic self-edge. Top shown,
Tawny Walnut.

Chair C-5465 – High Back,
Goldtone Finish (1963)
Legs, 1" tapered. Overall height, 34
½". Cover shown, No. 430 White.

Set: $350-500

Table T-8498 – Pedestal Base, Goldtone
Finish (1963)
48" round top (non-extension) on graceful
pedestal base. 1 ¾" plastic self-edge. Top
shown, White Velvet.

Chair C-5470 – High Back, Goldtone
Finish (1963)
Legs, 7/8". Overall height, 36". Cover
shown, No. 432 Red.

Set: $400-500

Table T-8480 – Pedestal Base, Goldtone Finish (1963) Top is 42" x 48" x 72" with two 12" leaves. Plastic self-edge. Top shown, Tawny Walnut.

Chair C-5466 – High Back, Goldtone Finish (1963) Legs, 1" tapered. Overall height, 34 ½". Cover shown, No. 382 White.

Set: $450-600

Table T-8484 – Goldtone Finish (1963) 30" x 40" x 48" top with 8" leaf. 1 ¾" tapered tubular legs. Top shown, White Flitter.

Chair C-5474 – Goldtone Finish (1963) Legs, 7/8". Overall height 31". Cover shown, No. 380 Tan.

Set: $250-300

Table T-8485 – Goldtone Finish (1963)
36" x 48" x 60" top with 12" leaf. 1 ½" tapered tubular legs.
Top shown, Brown/White Print.

Chair C-5475 – Goldtone Finish (1963)
Legs, 7/8". Overall height, 32 ½".

Set: $350-400

Table T-8501 – Goldtone Finish (1963)
42" round top extends to 42" x 60" oval with 18" leaf. Legs are 1 ½" tapered tubular. Top shown, Blond Cherry.

Chair C-5476 – Goldtone Finish (1963)
Legs, 7/8". Overall height, 32 ½". Cover shown, No. 362 Brown.

Set: $200-300

Table T-8486 – Goldtone Finish (1963)
36" x 48" x 72" top includes two 12" leaves. 1 ½" tapered tubular legs. Top shown, Sandstone Walnut.

Chair C-5475 – Goldtone Finish (1963)
Legs, 7/8". Overall height, 32 ½". Cover shown, No. 381 Gold.

Set: $400-500

Table T-8481 – Goldtone Finish (1963)
30" x 40" x 48" top with 8" leaf, as shown. Legs are 1 ¼" tapered tubular. Top shown, Champagne Walnut.

Chair C-5474 – Goldtone Finish (1963)
Legs, 7/8". Overall height, 31". Cover shown, No. 384 Beige.

Set: $250-300

Table T-8500 – Goldtone Finish (1963)
36" round top extends to 36" x 60" oval shape with two
12" leaves, as shown. Legs are 1 ½" tapered tubular. Top
shown, American Provincial Walnut.

Chair C-5434 – Goldtone Finish (1963)
Legs, 1" tapered. Overall height, 32". Cover shown, No.
412 Beige Dot and Dash.

Set: $250-350

Table T-8482 – Goldtone Finish (1963)
36" x 48" x 60" top with 12" leaf. Legs are 1 ½"
tapered tubular. Top shown, Tawny Walnut.

Chair C-5475 – Goldtone Finish (1963)
Legs, 7/8". Overall height, 32 ½". Cover shown,
No. 405 Tan.

Set: $250-350

48

Table T-8499 – Drop Leaf, Goldtone Finish (1963)
30" x 22" x 48" top. Gold colored, extruded aluminum edge banding. Legs are 1 ¼"
tapered tubular. Top shown, White Mahogany.

Chair C-5474 – Goldtone Finish (1963)
Legs, 7/8". Overall height, 31". Cover shown, No. 379 Turquoise.

Set: $150-250

Table T-8502 – Drop Leaf, Goldtone Finish (1963)
30" x 22" x 48" top. Gold colored, anodized, extruded aluminum banding. Legs are 1 ¾"
tapered tubular. Top shown, Sandstone Walnut.

Chair C-5467 – High Back, Goldtone Finish (1963)
Legs, 7/8". Overall height, 36". Cover shown, No. 400 White Stripe.

Set: $150-250

Table T-8469 – Narrow-Top Drop Leaf, Goldtone Finish (1963)
36" x 16" x 60" top (36" x 16" closed). Gold-colored anodized, extruded aluminum banding. Pull-out lever extends leg assemblies. Legs are 1 ¾" tapered tubular. Top shown, Tawny Walnut.

Chair C-5469 – High Back, Goldtone Finish (1963)
Legs, 7/8". Overall height, 36 ½". Cover shown, No. 406 White Stripe.

Set: $150-250

Table T-8514 – "Continental," White Enamel Finish (1964)
48" diameter round, non-extension top with tapered edge protected by an anodized gold colored, extruded aluminum banding. Height 26 ½". Tawny Walnut, White Brushstone, Toast Danish Walnut, and White Florentine Marble top patterns only. Also available in Goldtone finish.

Chair C-5488 – "Continental," Fiberglass Swivel, White Enamel Finish (1964) Smart, decorator styled shell of molded fiberglass in Coral, Parchment, Beige or Turquoise colors. Overall height 30". Also available in Goldtone finish.

Set: $700-900

Table T-8522 – Pedestal Base (1965)
42" diameter top (non extension) table topped with plastic self-edged White Florentine Marble patterned surface. Tubular frame finished in glossy Black with gold decals and gold colored metal ornamentation. Height 26 ½".

Chair C-5498 – High Back (1965)
Decorated hardwood back rail. Black welts. Overall height 43".

Set: $700-900

Table T-8536 – Pedestal Base (1965)
48" diameter top (non extension) table topped with plastic self-edged White Florentine Marble patterned surface. Tubular frame finished in glossy Black with gold decals and gold colored metal ornamentation. Height 26 ½".

Chair C-5509 – High Back (1965)
Gold colored metal back medallion and head trim on back and seat. Black welts. Overall height 41 ¼".

Set: $700-900

Table T-8536 – Pedestal Base (1965)
48" diameter top (non extension) table topped with plastic self-edged White Florentine Marble patterned surface. Tubular frame finished in glossy Black with gold decals and gold colored metal ornamentation. Height 26 ½".

Chair C-5510 – High Back (1965)
Gold colored metal back medallion. Black welts. Overall height 42 ¼".

Set: $700-900

Table T-8515 – Goldtone Finish (1965)
36" x 60" surfboard shaped, non-extension top.

Chair C-5490 – Swivel Chair, Goldtone Finish (1965)
Full upholstered, wrap-around back. Urethane foam cushioning in seat and back. Self-welts. Available with quilted upholstery cover. Overall height 33".

Set: $650-750

Table T-8511-SE – Goldtone Finish (1965)
42" diameter round, non-extension, self-edge top.

Chair C-5507 – Swivel Chair, Goldtone Finish (1965)
Full upholstered back and urethane foam cushioning in seat. Self-welts. Available with quilted upholstered cover. Overall height 33 ¾".

Set: $650-750

Table T-8513-SE – Goldtone Finish (1965)
48" diameter round, non-extension top with self-edge.

Chair C-5508 – Swivel Chair, Goldtone Finish (1965) Urethane foam cushioned seat and shaped upholstered back rest. Self-welts. Overall height 40".

Set: $700-800

Table T-8512-SE – White Enamel Finish (1965)
42" diameter round, non-extension, self-edge top.

Chair C-5489 –Swivel Chair, White Enamel Finish (1965)
Urethane foam seat cushioning with white extruded plastic welt. Decorative wrought iron backrest with circular cushion to match seat. Overall height 31 ½".

Set: $600-700

Table T-8524 – Pedestal Base Extension, Goldtone Finish (1965)
42" diameter round top, with plastic self-edge, extends to 42" x 60" oval, with 18" leaf. Height 29 ½".

Chair C-5503 – Goldtone Finish (1965)
Rolled-front seat cushion. Self-welts. Upholstered back rest with hardwood rail finished in rich Tawny Walnut. Legs 7/8". Overall height 31 ¾".

Set: $500-600

Table T-8525 – Pedestal Base Extension, Goldtone Finish (1965) 42" x 42" square top, curved sides, plastic self-edge, extends to 42" x 60" with 18" leaf. Height 29 ½".

Chair C-5468 – High Back, Goldtone Finish (1965) Shaped, upholstered back. Legs 7/8". Overall height 35".

Set: $450-550

Table T-8483 – Goldtone Finish (1965)
36" x 48" x 72" top includes two 12" leaves, as shown. Top is trimmed with anodized, gold-colored, extruded aluminum—a high quality banding with a finish that does not rub off, is easily cleaned, and stubbornly resistant to damage. Legs are 1 ½" tapered tubular.

Chair C-5475 – Goldtone Finish (1965)
No-mar back. Legs 7/8". Overall height 32 ½".

Set: $500-600

Table T-8532 – Goldtone Finish (1965)
30" x 40" x 48" top with 8" leaf, as shown. Top is trimmed with anodized, gold-colored, extruded aluminum—a high quality banding with a finish that does not rub off, is easily cleaned, and stubbornly resistant to damage. Legs are 1 ¼" tapered tubular.

Chair C-5475 – Goldtone Finish (1965)
No-mar back. Legs 7/8". Overall height 32 ½".'

Set: $400-500

Table T-3086 – Pedestal Base Extension, Chrome Finish (1966)
42" diameter round top, with plastic self-edge, extends to 42" x 60" oval as shown, with 18" extension leaf.

Chair C-1633 – Pedestal Base Swivel Chair, Chrome Finish (1966)
Box seat cushioned with urethane foam topper. Shaped, padded back rest. Self-welts. Available with channeled upholstery as shown. Self-aligning glides. Overall height 36 ½".

Set: $500-600

Table T-3087 – Pedestal Base Extension, Chrome Finish (1966)
42" x 42" square top, curved sides, plastic self-edge, extends to 42" x 60" with 18" extension leaf.

Chair C-1632 – High Back, Chrome Finish (1966)
Box seat and full height padded back rest. Self-welts. Available with channeled upholstery as shown. 7/8" tapered tubular legs. Self-aligning glides. Overall height 36 ½".

Set: $600-800

Table T-8543 – Pedestal Base Extension Table, Goldtone Finish (1966)
42" diameter round top, with plastic self-edge, extends to 42" x 60" oval as shown, with 18" extension leaf.

Chair C–5518 – Goldtone Finish (1966)
Box type seat cushion with self-welt. Padded back rest panel. 7/8" tapered legs. Overall height 32 ¾".

Set: $500-650

57

Table T-8544 – Pedestal Base Extension Table, Goldtone Finish (1966)
42" x 42" square top, curved sides, plastic self-edge, extends to 42" x 60" with 18" leaf as shown.

Chair C-5468 – High Back, Goldtone Finish (1966)
Shaped, upholstered back. Legs 7/8". Overall height 35".

Set: $450-550

Table T-8546 – Pedestal Base, Goldtone Finish (1966)
42" diameter round, non-extension, self-edge top.

Chair C-5520 – Swivel Chair, Goldtone Finish (1966)
Full upholstered back. Self-welts. Available with channeled upholstery cover. Overall height 35 ½".

Set: $500-600

Table T-8547 – Pedestal Base, Goldtone Finish (1966)
48" diameter round, non-extension, self-edge top.

Chair C-5521 – Swivel Chair, Goldtone Finish (1966)
Full upholstered wrap-around back. Urethane foam cushioning in seat and back.
Self-welts. Available with channeled upholstery as shown. Overall height 35".

Set: $500-650

Table T-8549 – Pedestal Base, Black Enamel Finish (1966)
48" diameter top (non extension) table topped with plastic self-edged White Florentine Marble patterned surface. Tubular frame finished in glossy Black with gold decals and gold colored metal ornamentation. Height 26 ½".

Chair C-5525 – High Back, Black Enamel Finish (1966)
Back posts ornamented with gold colored metal finials. Overall height 40".

Set: $450-550

Table T-8518 – "Plymouth House," Harvest Table, Bronze Finish (1966)
Top 36" x 48" with both leaves raised. Plastic self-edge top. 1 ½" tapered legs. Pull-out legs to support leaves.

Chair C-5477 – "Plymouth House," Bronze Finish (1966)
Hardwood back rest decorated with quaint Early American floral motif and gold colored finials. Legs 7/8". Bronze extruded plastic welts.

Bench B-5479 – "Plymouth House," Bronze Finish (1966)
Seat 40 ½" wide, seats two.

Set (table and chairs): $300-400
Bench: $200-250

Table T-8530 – "Plymouth House,"
Harvest Table, Bronze Finish (1966)
Top 42" x 60" with both leaves raised. Plastic
self-edge. 1 ¾" tapered legs. Pull-out legs to
support leaves. Full-length, brass plated
piano hinge.

Chair C-5524 – "Plymouth House,"
Bronze Finish (1966)
Hardwood back rail decorated with Early
American eagle motif. Padded back rest
panel. Back posts trimmed with gold colored
metal finials. Legs 7/8".

Set: $400-500

Table T-8478-SE –
"Plymouth House,"
Bronze Finish (1966)
Top 36" x 48" x 60"
with 12" extension leaf.
Tapered, plastic self-
edge top. Leaf hanger
for self-storing of leaf.
Also available with two
12" leaves.

Chair C-5522 –
"Plymouth House,"
Bronze Finish (1966)
Shaped, maple
finished, hardwood
back rail with Early
American motif. Legs
7/8". Bronze extruded
plastic welt.

Set: $400-500

Table T-8479-SE – "Plymouth House," Bronze Finish (1966)
42" round top extends to 42" x 60" oval as shown. Tapered, plastic self-edge.

Chair C-5523 – "Plymouth House," Bronze Finish (1966)
Hardwood back rail decorated with Early American motif. Padded back rest panel. Back posts have gold colored metal caps. Legs 7/8".

Set: $350-450

Table T-8494-SE – Goldtone Finish (1966)
Top 42" x 48" x 72", including two 12" extension leaves as shown.

Chair C-5514 – High Back, Goldtone Finish (1966)
Modern styled metal back rest. Self-welt on seat cushion. 7/8" tapered legs. Overall height 36 ½".

Set: $400-500

Table T-8555 – Pedestal Base Extension Table, Goldtone Finish (1967)
42" x 48" oval top extends to 42" x 60" as shown with 12" extension leaf in place. 1 ¾" thick plastic laminated, self-edge top surface. Pedestal columns are 2 ½" diameter. Also available with two 12" extension leaves.

Chair C-5538 – Pedestal Base Swivel Chair, Goldtone Finish (1967)
Box seat cushioned with urethane foam topper. Shaped, padded back rest. Overall height 35".

Set: $500-600

Table T-8553 – Pedestal Base Extension Table, Goldtone Finish (1967)
42" diameter round top, extends to 42" x 60" oval as shown with 18" extension leaf. Tapered, plastic laminated self-edge to match top surface. Tapered pedestal base legs. Also available with two 15" extension leaves.

Chair C-5530 – High Back (1967)
Legs 7/8". Rolled front seat cushion and deep, tapered back rest. Overall height 33 ½".

Set: $400-500

Table T-8556-A – Double Pedestal Base, Goldtone Finish (1969)
42" x 48" oval top extends to 42" x 72" with two 12" leaves in place, as shown. 1 ¾" thick plastic laminated, self-edge top surface. Pedestal columns are 2 ¼" diameter tubing. Automatic self adjusting metal floor guides.

Chair C-5552 – Pedestal Base Swivel Chair, Goldtone Finish (1969)
Wide, contoured bucket seat cushion 17 ½" x 16 ¾". Extra wide and roomy, upholstered back rest. Ball bearing swivel mechanism. Overall height 34 ½".

Chair C-5551 – Pedestal Base Swivel Chair, Goldtone Finish (straight leg frame) (1969)
Has straight leg frame as shown, otherwise same as C-5552.

Set: $600-700

Table T-8543-A – Pedestal Base Extension Table, Goldtone Finish (1969)
42" diameter round top with plastic laminated self-edge, extends to 42" x 60" oval, as shown, with 18" extension leaf in place. Pedestal column is 2 ¼" diameter tubing. Automatic self-adjusting metal floor glides. Equipped with easy acting ratchet extension top.

Chair C-5540 – Pedestal Base Swivel Chair, Goldtone Finish (1969)
Box type seat 17 ¾" x 17", cushioned with thick urethane foam. Shaped and fully upholstered back rest. Wrap around seat and back frame. Ball bearing swivel mechanism. Overall height 36".

Set: $500-600

Table T-8555-A – Double Pedestal Base Extension Table, Goldtone Finish (1969)
42" x 48" oval top extends to 42" x 60" with 12" extension leaf in place, as shown. 1 ¾" thick plastic laminated, self-edge top surface. Pedestal columns are 2 ¼" diameter tubing. Automatic self adjusting metal floor glides.

Chair C-5552 – Pedestal Base Swivel Chair Goldtone Finish (1969)
Wide, contoured bucket seat cushion 17 ½" x 16 ¾". Extra wide and roomy, upholstered back rest. Ball bearing swivel mechanism. Overall height 34 ½".

Set: $450-550

Table T-8558-A – Pedestal Base Extension Table, Goldtone Finish (1969)
42" diameter round top with 1 ¾" plastic laminated self-edge, extends to 42" x 60" oval with 18" extension leaf, as shown. Automatic self adjusting metal floor glides. Equipped with easy-acting ratchet extension top.

Chair C-5541 – Pedestal Base Swivel Chair, Goldtone Finish (1969)
Wide, contoured bucket seat cushion, 17 ½" x 16 ¾". Plastic laminated back rest in Brown Planked Walnut pattern only. Ball bearing swivel mechanism. Overall height 33".

Set: $500-600

Table T-8490-B – Goldtone Finish (1969)
42" x 60" x 96" top with two 18" extension leaves in place, as shown. 1 ¾" thick plastic laminated self-edge with ratchet type extension slides to make it easier to open and close top when using extension leaves. Legs are 1 ¾" tapered, with permanently knurled leg decoration. Top gets extra support at center from additional leg with automatic self adjusting metal glide. Brown Planked Walnut and Imperial Walnut tops only.

Chair C-5543 – High Back, Goldtone Finish (1969)
Thickly upholstered rolled front seat cushion, 16 ¼" x 15 ¾". Extra high upholstered back rest with arched top. Overall height 35".

Set: $700-800

Table T-8489 – Goldtone Finish (1969)
42" x 48" x 72" top with two 12" extension leaves in place, as shown. 1 ¾" thick plastic laminated self-edge. 1 ¾" diameter tapered legs, with permanently knurled decoration.

Chair C-5515 – High Back, Goldtone Finish (1969)
Thickly upholstered, box type seat cushion 17" x 16 ¾". High, decorator styled upholstered back rest. Tapered legs. Overall height 36 ½".

Set: $600-700

Table T-8487 – Goldtone Finish (1969)
36" x 48" x 60" top with 12" extension leaf in place, as shown. 1 ¾" thick plastic laminated self-edge. 1 ¾" diameter tapered legs with permanently knurled decoration. Leaf hanger for self storing of extension leaf. Also available with two 12" extension leaves.

Chair C-5547 – High Back, Goldtone Finish (1969)
Thickly upholstered box type seat cushion 16 ¾" x 16 ¼". Upholstered back rest topped with decorative wood back rail finished in Gunstock Walnut only. Tapered legs. Overall height 37 ½".

Set: $400-500

Table T-8474-SE – Goldtone Finish (1969)
36" x 48" x 60" top with 12" extension leaf in place, as shown. Leaf hanger for self storing of extension leaf. Top surface has tapered plastic laminate self-edge. Legs are 1 ¾" diameter, double tapered at top and bottom. Also available with two 12" extension leaves.

Chair C-5516 – High Back, Goldtone Finish (1969)
Contoured upholstered seat cushion 17 ½" x 16 ¾". Plastic laminated back rest in Brown Planked Walnut pattern only. Overall height 34".

Set: $500-600

Table T-8494-SE – Goldtone Finish (1969)
42" x 48" x 72" top with two 12" extension leaves in place, as shown. Top surface has tapered, plastic laminated self-edge. Legs are 1 ¾" diameter, double tapered at top and bottom.

Chair C-5553 – High Back, Goldtone Finish (1969)
Thickly upholstered box type seat cushion 16" x 16 ¼". Upholstered back rest. Tapered legs. Overall height 35".

Set: $400-500

Table T-8475-SE – Goldtone Finish (1969)
42" diameter round top extends to 42" x 60" oval as shown, with 18" extension leaf in place. Top surface has tapered, plastic laminated self-edge. Legs are 1 ¾" diameter, double tapered at top and bottom. Also available with two 15" extension leaves.

Chair C-5528 – Goldtone Finish (1969)
Thickly upholstered box type seat cushion 17" x 15 ¾". Gold colored metal grill in tubular back frame. Overall height 32".

Set: $350-450

Table T-8517-SE – Goldtone Finish (1969)
36" diameter round top extends to 36" x 60" oval as shown, with two
12" extension leaves in place. Top surface has tapered, plastic laminated
self-edge. Legs are 1 ¾" diameter, double tapered at top and bottom.

Chair C-5499 – High Back, Goldtone Finish (1969)
Thickly upholstered, box type seat cushion 16 ¾" x 16 ¼". Upholstered
back rest. Tapered legs. Overall height 36 ½".

Set: $400-500

Table T-8559-SE – Goldtone Finish (1969)
36" x 48" oval top, extends to 36" x 60" oval as shown, with 12" extension leaf in place.
Top has tapered plastic laminated self-edge. Legs are 1 ¾" diameter, double tapered at
top and bottom.

Chair C-5545 – High Back, Goldtone Finish (1969)
Thickly upholstered box type seat cushion, 16 ¼" x 15 ¾". Gunstock Walnut finished
wood back rail with gold colored metal wire grill. Overall height 34".

Set: $300-400

Table T-8559-SE – Goldtone Finish (1969)
36" x 48" oval top, extends to 36" x 60" oval as shown, with 12" extension leaf in place. Top has tapered plastic laminated self-edge. Legs are 1 ¾" diameter, double tapered at top and bottom.

Chair C-5555 – Ladder Back Chair, Goldtone Finish (1969)
Thickly upholstered box type seat cushion 16" x 16 ¼". Back rail and slats of wood with Brown Planked Walnut finish only as shown. Legs are tapered. Overall height 33". Also available in Avocado finish (C-5558, see page 74).

Set: $350-450

Table T-8493-SE – Goldtone Finish (1969)
30" x 40" x 48" top with 8" extension leaf as shown. Top has tapered plastic laminated self-edge. Legs are 1 ¾" diameter, double tapered at top and bottom. Leaf hanger for self storing of extension leaf.

Chair C-5554 – High Back, Goldtone Finish (1969)
Thickly upholstered box type seat cushion 17" x 16 ¼". Heart shaped, upholstered back rest. Legs are tapered. Overall height 33".

Set: $350-450

Table T-8507 – Goldtone Finish (1969)
42" x 48" x 72" top with two 12" extension leaves in place, as shown. Top is 1 ½" thick with plastic laminated self-edge. Legs are 1 ½" diameter, tapered at bottom. Also available in Avocado finish.

Chair C-5534 – High Back, Goldtone Finish (1969)
Thickly upholstered rolled front seat cushion 16 ¼" x 15 ¾". Upholstered back rest with gold colored metal rod decoration. Overall height 36 ½".

Set: $400-600

Table T-8567 – Avocado Finish (1969)
42" round top extends to 42" x 60" oval as shown, with 18" extension leaf in place. Top is 1 ½" thick with plastic laminated self-edge. Legs are 1 ½" diameter, tapered at bottom. Also available in Goldtone finish (T-8501, *see next picture*).

Chair C-5558 – Ladder Back Chair, Avocado Finish (1969)
Thickly upholstered box type seat cushion, 16" x 16 ¼". Back rail and slats of wood with natural finish only, as shown. Legs are tapered. Overall height 33". Also available in Goldtone finish (C-5555, see page 72).

Set: $350-400

Table T-8501 – Goldtone Finish (1969)
42" round top extends to 42" x 60" oval, with 18" extension leaf in place, as shown. Top is
1 ½" thick with plastic laminated self-edge. Legs are 1 ½" diameter, tapered at bottom.
Also available in Avocado finish (T-8567, see previous picture).

Chair C-5544 – High Back, Goldtone Finish (1969)
Thickly upholstered box type seat cushion 17" x 16 ¼". Shaped, plastic laminated back
rest in Country Walnut pattern only. Overall height 35 ½".

Set: $350-500

Table T-8486 – Goldtone Finish (1969)
36" x 48" x 72" top with two 12" extension leaves in place, as shown. Top is
1 ½" thick with plastic laminated self-edge. Legs are 1 ½" diameter, tapered
at bottom. Also available in Avocado finish.

Chair C-5481 – "Heywoodite" Chair, Goldtone Finish (1969)
Seat, 16 ½" x 15 ½", and back of "Heywoodite," exclusive solid molded
plastic—waterproof, fireproof, does not chip, crack, or scratch easily. Color is
permanently molded in. Available in choice of Wedgwood (as shown),
Flamingo, Cocoa, or Off-White. Overall height 32".

Set: $400-500

Table T-8485 – Goldtone Finish (1969)
36" x 48" x 60" top with 12" extension leaf in place as shown. Top is 1 ½" thick with plastic laminated self-edge.
Legs are 1 ½" diameter tapered at bottom. Also available in Avocado finish.

Chair C-5527 – Goldtone Finish (1969)
Thickly upholstered box type seat cushion 16" x 15 ¾". Deep, upholstered back rest. Overall height 32".

Set: $350-450

Table T-8550 – Goldtone Finish (1969)
36" x 36" square top, as shown, extends to 36" x 60" with two 12" leaves in place. Top is 1 ½" thick with plastic laminated self-edge. Legs are 1 ½" diameter, tapered at bottom. Also available in Avocado finish.

Chair C-5502 – Goldtone Finish (1969)
Thickly upholstered box type seat cushion 16" x 16 ¼". Elegantly designed, gold colored metal back rest with grill solidly welded into back frame. Tapered legs. Overall height 32 ¼".

Set: $300-400

Table T-8560 – "Plymouth House," Bronze Finish (1969)
36" x 48" oval shape top extends to 36" x 60" oval as shown, with 12" leaf in place. Top is 1 ¾" thick with plastic laminated self-edge. Legs are 1 ¾" diameter, tapered at bottom.

Chair C-5549 – "Plymouth House," Bronze Finish (1969)
Thickly upholstered box type seat cushion 16 ¼" x 15 ¾". Maple finished wood back rail and turned spindles. Overall height 34 ½".

Set: $250-350

Table T-8560 – "Plymouth House," Bronze Finish (1969)
36" x 48" oval shape top extends to 36" x 60" oval as shown, with 12" leaf in place. Top is 1 ½" thick with plastic laminated self-edge. Legs are 1 ¾" diameter, tapered at bottom.

Chair C-5550 – "Plymouth House," Bronze Finish (1969)
Thickly upholstered box type seat cushion 16 ¼" x 15 ¾". Shaped, maple finished wood back rail with tubular bronze finished metal spindles. Overall height 34".

Set: $250-350

Table T-8448-A – Drop Leaf, Goldtone Finish (1969)
42" x 25" x 84" top as shown, including 18" extension leaf, folds down to 42" x 25" as shown in small illustration. Fully extended, table seats eight. Plastic laminated self-edge all around top and drop leaves. Handy pull-out lever to extend leg assemblies. Legs are 1 ¾" diameter, tapered at bottom. Full length piano hinges keep drop leaves permanently straight.

Chair C-5533 – High Back, Goldtone Finish (1969)
Thickly upholstered box type seat cushion 16" x 15 ¾". Upholstered, decorator styled back rest. Overall height 35".

Set: $500-600

Table T-8561 – "Plymouth House," Bronze Finish (1969)
42" round top extends to 42" x 60" with 18" extension leaf in place, as shown. Top is 1 ½" thick with plastic laminated self-edge. Legs are 1 ¾" diameter, tapered at bottom.

Chair C-5548 – "Plymouth House," Bronze Finish (1969)
Thickly upholstered box type seat cushion 16 ¼" x 15 ¾". Upholstered back rest with maple finished wood back rail. Overall height 33 ½".

Set: $250-350

Table T-8528-A – Drop Leaf, Goldtone Finish (1969)
36" x 25" x 72" top, including 12" extension leaf. Plastic laminated self-edge all around top and drop leaves. Handy pull out lever to extend leg assemblies. Legs are 1 ¾" diameter, tapered at bottom. Full length piano hinges keep drop leaves permanently straight.

Chair C-5556 – Goldtone Finish (1969)
Thickly upholstered box type seat cushion 16" x 16 ¼". Back rest of tubular metal, with spindles solidly welded into frame. Tapered legs. Overall height 32 ¾".

Set: $200-250

Table T-8552 – Drop Leaf, Goldtone Finish (1969)
42" x 25" x 72" top, including 12" extension leaf. Plastic laminated self-edge all around top and drop leaves. Legs are 1 ¾", tapered at bottom. Handy pull out lever for extending leg assemblies. Full length piano hinges keep drop leaves permanently straight.

Chair C-5537 – High Back, Goldtone Finish (1969)
Thickly upholstered box type seat cushion 16" x 15 ¾". Plastic laminated back rest in Brown Planked Walnut pattern only. Overall height 33 ½".

Set: $250-300

Table T-8502-A – Drop Leaf, Goldtone Finish (1969)
30" x 22" x 48" top. Gold colored, anodized extruded aluminum edge banding all around top and drop leaves. Legs 1 ¾", tapered at bottom. Leg assemblies pull out to fully support drop leaves. Full length piano hinges keep drop leaves permanently straight. Also available with plastic laminated self-edges all around top and drop leaves.

Chair C-5546 – High Back, Goldtone Finish (1969)
Thickly upholstered box type seat cushion 16 ¼" x 15 ¾". Wood back rail and decorative slats finished in Gunstock Walnut only. Overall height 34 ½".

Set: $200-250

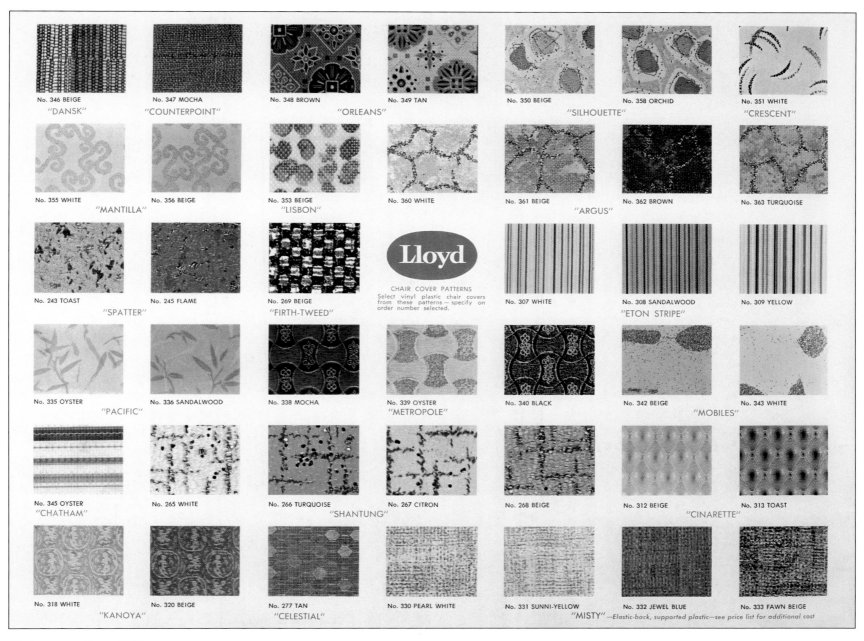

No. 346 BEIGE — "DANSK"
No. 347 MOCHA — "COUNTERPOINT"
No. 348 BROWN — "ORLEANS"
No. 349 TAN
No. 350 BEIGE — "SILHOUETTE"
No. 358 ORCHID
No. 351 WHITE — "CRESCENT"

No. 355 WHITE — "MANTILLA"
No. 356 BEIGE
No. 353 BEIGE — "LISBON"
No. 360 WHITE
No. 361 BEIGE — "ARGUS"
No. 362 BROWN
No. 363 TURQUOISE

No. 243 TOAST — "SPATTER"
No. 245 FLAME
No. 269 BEIGE — "FIRTH-TWEED"

Lloyd
CHAIR COVER PATTERNS
Select vinyl plastic chair covers from these patterns — specify on order number selected.

No. 307 WHITE
No. 308 SANDALWOOD — "ETON STRIPE"
No. 309 YELLOW

No. 335 OYSTER — "PACIFIC"
No. 336 SANDALWOOD
No. 338 MOCHA
No. 339 OYSTER — "METROPOLE"
No. 340 BLACK
No. 342 BEIGE — "MOBILES"
No. 343 WHITE

No. 345 OYSTER — "CHATHAM"
No. 265 WHITE
No. 266 TURQUOISE — "SHANTUNG"
No. 267 CITRON
No. 268 BEIGE
No. 312 BEIGE — "CINARETTE"
No. 313 TOAST

No. 318 WHITE — "KANOYA"
No. 320 BEIGE
No. 277 TAN — "CELESTIAL"
No. 330 PEARL WHITE
No. 331 SUNNI-YELLOW — "MISTY"
No. 332 JEWEL BLUE
No. 333 FAWN BEIGE

"MISTY" —Elastic-back, supported plastic—see price list for additional cost

Chair cover patterns, 1961.

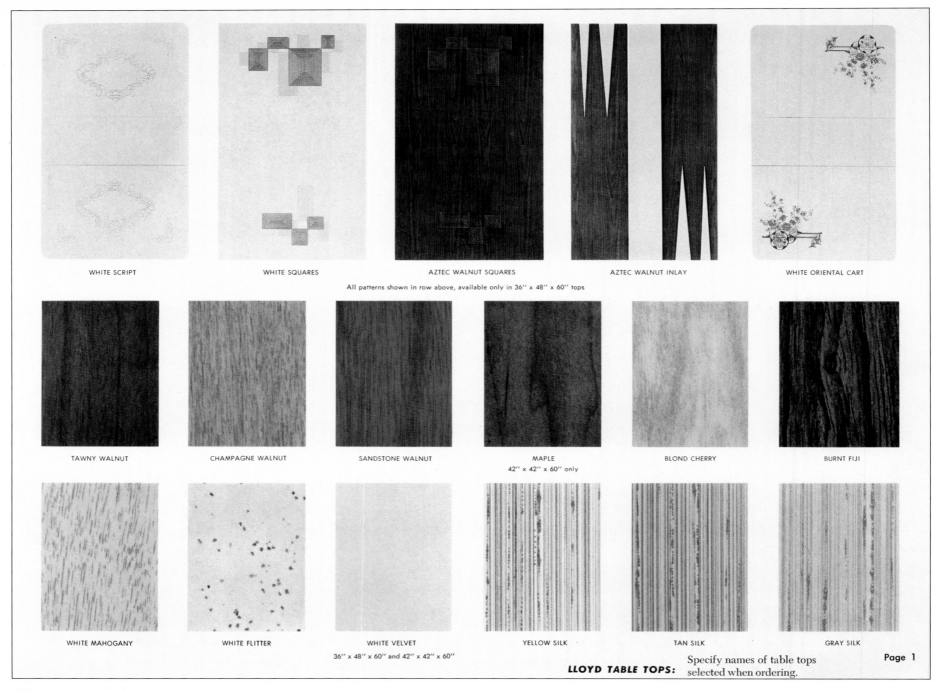

WHITE SCRIPT

WHITE SQUARES

AZTEC WALNUT SQUARES

AZTEC WALNUT INLAY

WHITE ORIENTAL CART

All patterns shown in row above, available only in 36'' x 48'' x 60'' tops

TAWNY WALNUT

CHAMPAGNE WALNUT

SANDSTONE WALNUT

MAPLE
42'' x 42'' x 60'' only

BLOND CHERRY

BURNT FIJI

WHITE MAHOGANY

WHITE FLITTER

WHITE VELVET
36'' x 48'' x 60'' and 42'' x 42'' x 60''

YELLOW SILK

TAN SILK

GRAY SILK

LLOYD TABLE TOPS: Specify names of table tops selected when ordering.

Page 1

Tabletop patterns, 1961.

84

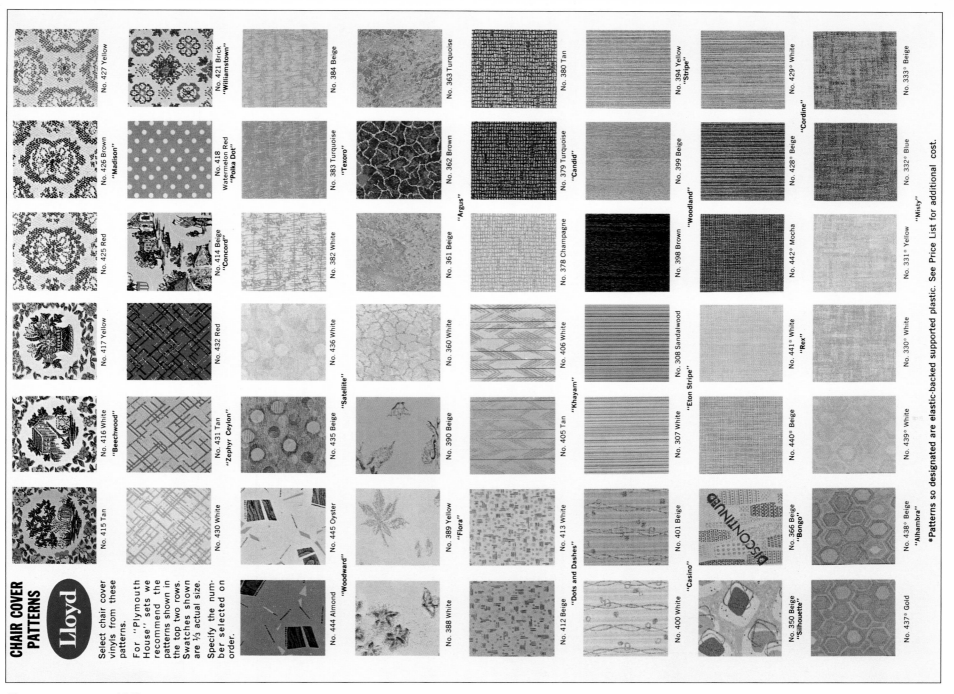

CHAIR COVER PATTERNS

Lloyd

Select chair cover vinyls from these patterns.

For "Plymouth House" sets we recommend the patterns shown in the top two rows. Swatches shown are 1/3 actual size.

Specify the number selected on order.

No. 427 Yellow
No. 421 Brick "Williamstown"
No. 384 Beige
No. 363 Turquoise
No. 380 Tan
No. 394 Yellow "Stripe"
No. 429 White "Cordine"
No. 333° Beige

No. 426 Brown "Madison"
No. 418 Watermelon Red "Polka Dot"
No. 383 Turquoise "Texoro"
No. 362 Brown
No. 379 Turquoise "Candid"
No. 399 Beige "Woodland"
No. 428° Beige
No. 332° Blue "Misty"

No. 425 Red
No. 414 Beige "Concord"
No. 382 White
No. 361 Beige "Argus"
No. 378 Champagne
No. 398 Brown "Eton Stripe"
No. 442° Mocha
No. 331° Yellow

No. 417 Yellow
No. 432 Red
No. 436 White "Satellite"
No. 360 White
No. 406 White "Khayam"
No. 308 Sandalwood
No. 441° White "Rex"
No. 330° White

No. 416 White "Beechwood"
No. 431 Tan "Zephyr Ceylon"
No. 435 Beige
No. 390 Beige
No. 405 Tan
No. 307 White
No. 440° Beige
No. 439° White "Alhambra"

No. 415 Tan
No. 430 White "Woodward"
No. 445 Oyster
No. 389 Yellow "Flora"
No. 413 White "Dots and Dashes"
No. 401 Beige "Casino"
No. 366 Beige "Bongo"
No. 438° Beige

No. 444 Almond
No. 388 White
No. 412 Beige
No. 400 White
No. 350 Beige "Silhouette"
No. 437° Gold

DISCONTINUED

*Patterns so designated are elastic-backed supported plastic. See Price List for additional cost.

Chair cover patterns, 1963.

85

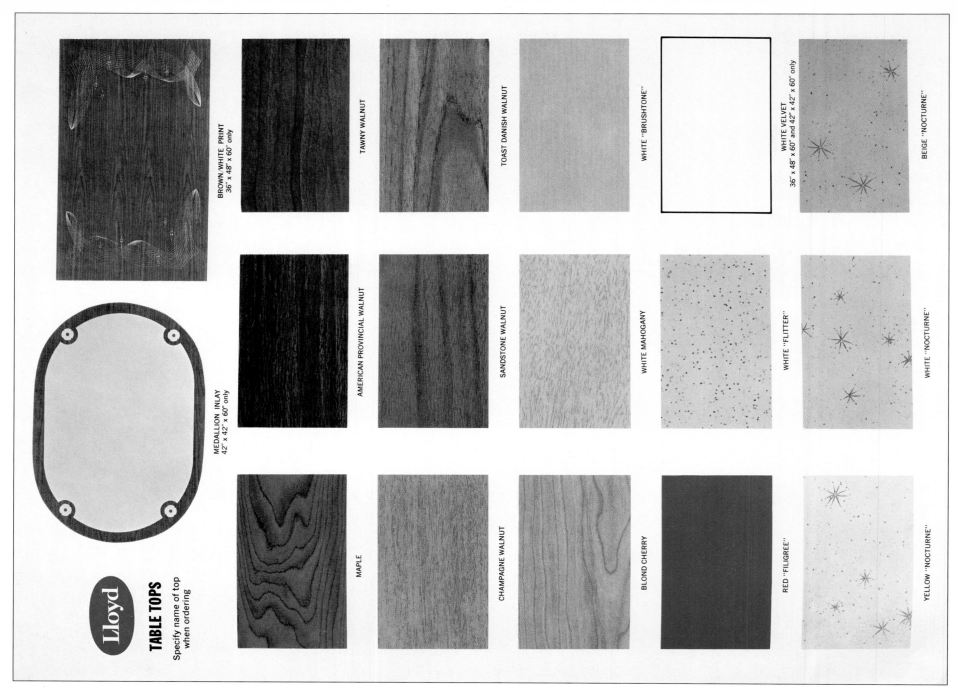

Lloyd

TABLE TOPS

Specify name of top when ordering

MEDALLION INLAY
42″ x 42″ x 60″ only

BROWN "WHITE PRINT
36″ x 48″ x 60″ only

AMERICAN PROVINCIAL WALNUT

TAWNY WALNUT

SANDSTONE WALNUT

TOAST DANISH WALNUT

WHITE MAHOGANY

WHITE "BRUSHTONE"

WHITE VELVET
36″ x 48″ x 60″ and 42″ x 42″ x 60″ only

WHITE "FLITTER"

BEIGE "NOCTURNE"

WHITE "NOCTURNE"

MAPLE

CHAMPAGNE WALNUT

BLOND CHERRY

RED "FILIGREE"

YELLOW "NOCTURNE"

Tabletop patterns, 1963.

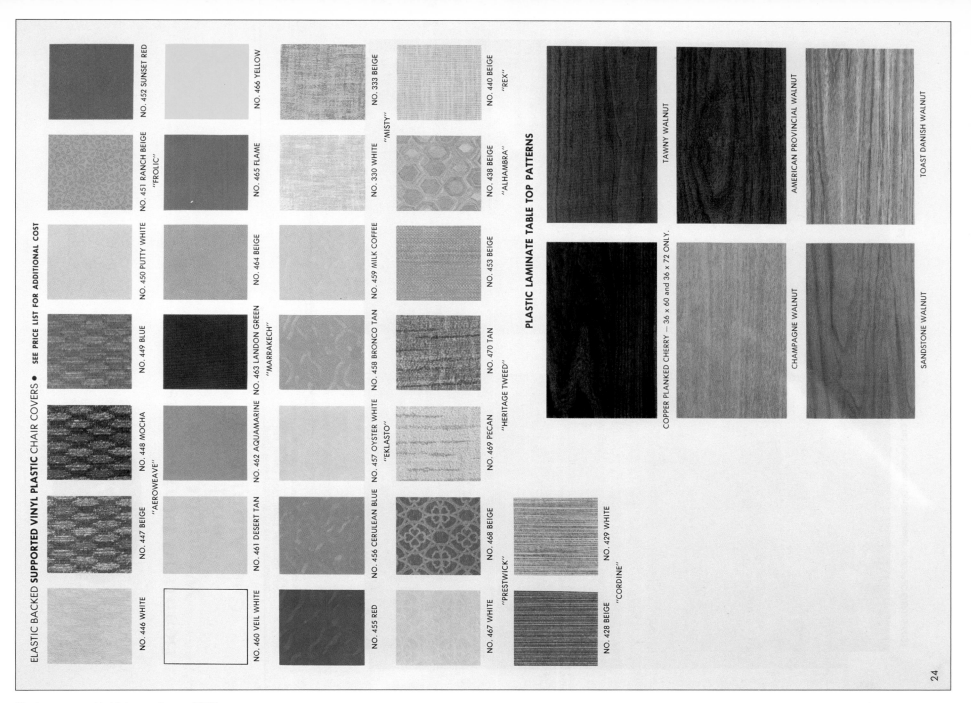

ELASTIC BACKED **SUPPORTED VINYL PLASTIC** CHAIR COVERS ● SEE PRICE LIST FOR ADDITIONAL COST

NO. 452 SUNSET RED

NO. 451 RANCH BEIGE "FROLIC"

NO. 450 PUTTY WHITE

NO. 449 BLUE

NO. 448 MOCHA "AEROWEAVE"

NO. 447 BEIGE

NO. 446 WHITE

NO. 460 VEIL WHITE

NO. 466 YELLOW

NO. 465 FLAME

NO. 464 BEIGE

NO. 463 LANDON GREEN "MARRAKECH"

NO. 462 AQUAMARINE

NO. 461 DESERT TAN

NO. 455 RED

NO. 333 BEIGE "MISTY"

NO. 330 WHITE

NO. 459 MILK COFFEE

NO. 458 BRONCO TAN

NO. 457 OYSTER WHITE "EKLASTO"

NO. 456 CERULEAN BLUE

NO. 467 WHITE

NO. 440 BEIGE "REX"

NO. 438 BEIGE "ALHAMBRA"

NO. 453 BEIGE

NO. 470 TAN "HERITAGE TWEED"

NO. 469 PECAN

NO. 468 BEIGE "PRESTWICK"

NO. 429 WHITE

NO. 428 BEIGE "CORDINE"

PLASTIC LAMINATE TABLE TOP PATTERNS

TAWNY WALNUT

AMERICAN PROVINCIAL WALNUT

TOAST DANISH WALNUT

COPPER PLANKED CHERRY — 36 x 60 and 36 x 72 ONLY.

CHAMPAGNE WALNUT

SANDSTONE WALNUT

24

Chair cover and tabletop patterns, 1964.

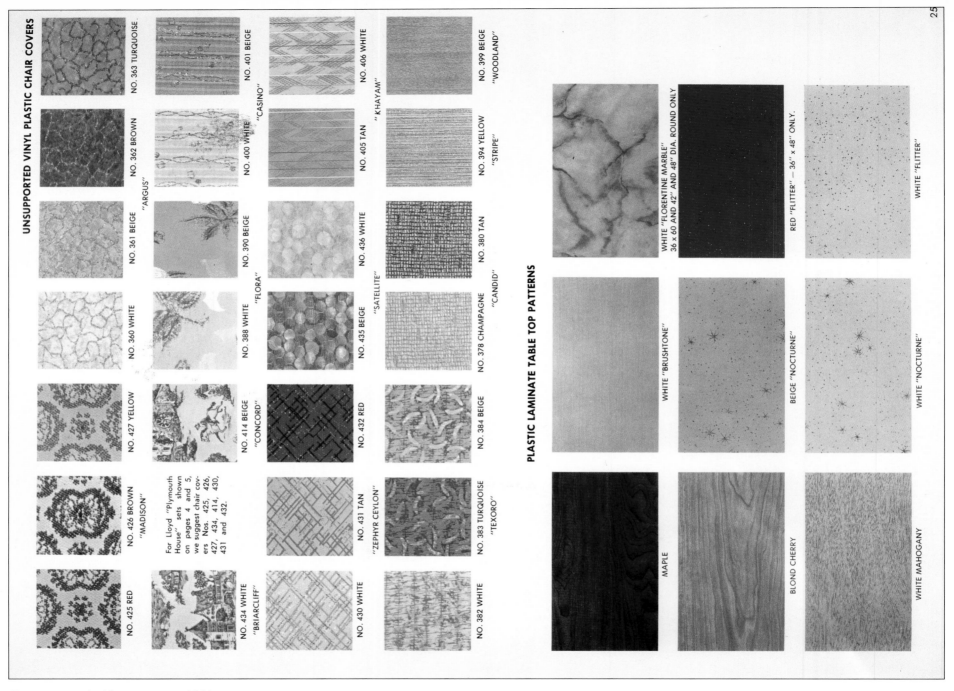

UNSUPPORTED VINYL PLASTIC CHAIR COVERS

NO. 363 TURQUOISE.

NO. 401 BEIGE
"CASINO"

NO. 406 WHITE
"KHAYAM"

NO. 399 BEIGE
"WOODLAND"

NO. 362 BROWN
"ARGUS"

NO. 400 WHITE

NO. 405 TAN

NO. 394 YELLOW
"STRIPE"

NO. 361 BEIGE

NO. 390 BEIGE
"FLORA"

NO. 436 WHITE
"SATELLITE"

NO. 380 TAN

NO. 360 WHITE

NO. 388 WHITE

NO. 435 BEIGE

NO. 378 CHAMPAGNE
"CANDID"

NO. 427 YELLOW

NO. 414 BEIGE
"CONCORD"

NO. 432 RED

NO. 384 BEIGE

NO. 426 BROWN
"MADISON"

For Lloyd "Plymouth House" sets shown on pages 4 and 5, we suggest chair covers Nos. 425, 426, 427, 434, 414, 430, 431 and 432.

NO. 431 TAN
"ZEPHYR CEYLON"

NO. 383 TURQUOISE
"TEXORO"

NO. 425 RED

NO. 434 WHITE
"BRIARCLIFF"

NO. 430 WHITE

NO. 382 WHITE

PLASTIC LAMINATE TABLE TOP PATTERNS

WHITE "FLORENTINE MARBLE"
36 x 60 AND 42" AND 48" DIA. ROUND ONLY

RED "FLITTER" — 36" x 48" ONLY.

WHITE "FLITTER"

WHITE "BRUSHTONE"

BEIGE "NOCTURNE"

WHITE "NOCTURNE"

MAPLE

BLOND CHERRY

WHITE MAHOGANY

Chair cover and tabletop patterns, 1964.

ELASTIC BACKED SUPPORTED VINYL PLASTIC CHAIR COVERS

"MISTY"				"CAMILLE"			
No. 330 White	No. 333 Beige	No. 475 Persimmon	No. 476 Champagne	No. 477 Beige	No. 478 Olive	No. 479 Turquoise	No. 480 Gold

"MARRAKECH"				"DAMASCIENE"			
No. 460 Veil White	No. 461 Desert Tan	No. 462 Aquamarine	No. 493 Pearl	No. 494 Gold	No. 495 Emerald	No. 496 Coral	No. 497 Avocado

"MARRAKECH"			"ALHAMBRA"			"MANGROVE"	
No. 463 Landon Green	No. 464 Beige	No. 465 Flame	No. 437 Gold	No. 438 Beige	No. 439 White	No. 490 Blue	No. 491 Brown

"MARRAKECH"			"ELITE"			"TIKI"	
No. 466 Yellow	No. 471 Black	No. 472 Cherry	No. 498 Beige	No. 499 White	No. 500 Beige	No. 501 Autumn	No. 502 Gold

"FANFARE"			"HARMONY"			"AVON"	
No. 503 White	No. 504 Fawn	No. 506 White	No. 507 Beige	No. 508 Gold	No. 510 White	No. 511 Beige	No. 512 Mocha

Chair cover patterns, 1965.

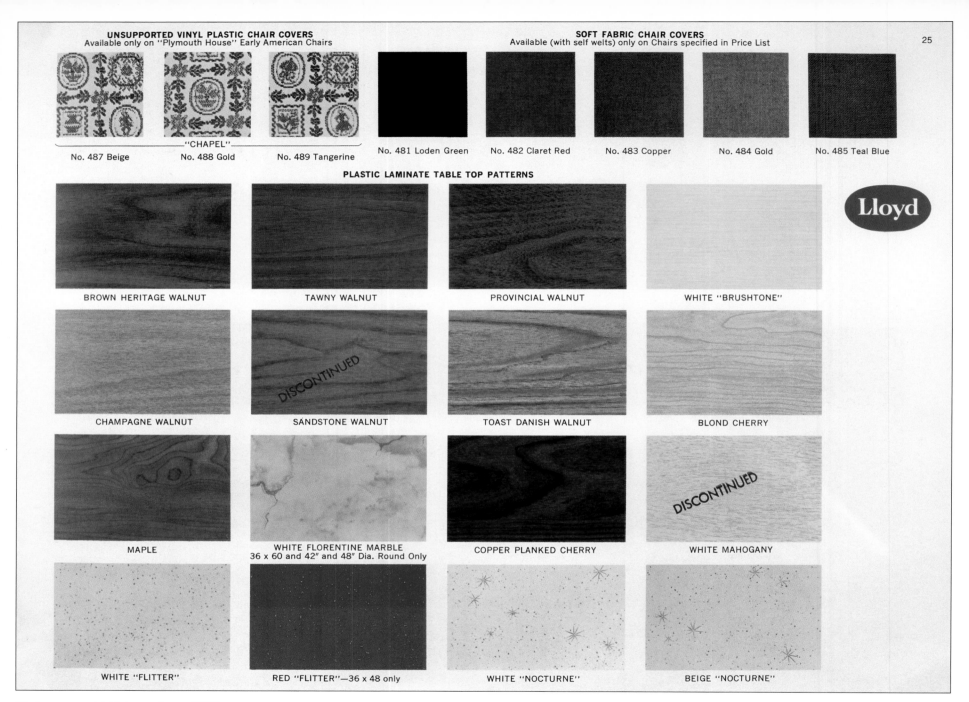

UNSUPPORTED VINYL PLASTIC CHAIR COVERS
Available only on "Plymouth House" Early American Chairs

SOFT FABRIC CHAIR COVERS
Available (with self welts) only on Chairs specified in Price List

"CHAPEL"

No. 487 Beige   No. 488 Gold   No. 489 Tangerine

No. 481 Loden Green   No. 482 Claret Red   No. 483 Copper   No. 484 Gold   No. 485 Teal Blue

PLASTIC LAMINATE TABLE TOP PATTERNS

BROWN HERITAGE WALNUT   TAWNY WALNUT   PROVINCIAL WALNUT   WHITE "BRUSHTONE"

CHAMPAGNE WALNUT   SANDSTONE WALNUT *(DISCONTINUED)*   TOAST DANISH WALNUT   BLOND CHERRY

MAPLE   WHITE FLORENTINE MARBLE 36 x 60 and 42" and 48" Dia. Round Only   COPPER PLANKED CHERRY   WHITE MAHOGANY *(DISCONTINUED)*

WHITE "FLITTER"   RED "FLITTER"—36 x 48 only   WHITE "NOCTURNE"   BEIGE "NOCTURNE"

Lloyd

Chair cover and tabletop patterns, 1965.

ELASTIC BACKED SUPPORTED VINYL PLASTIC CHAIR COVERS

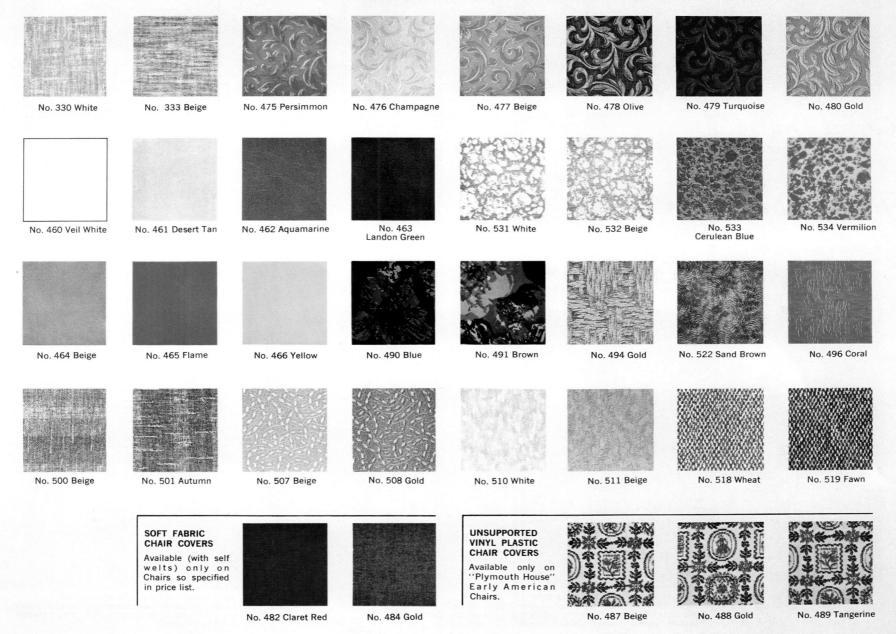

No. 330 White	No. 333 Beige	No. 475 Persimmon	No. 476 Champagne	No. 477 Beige	No. 478 Olive	No. 479 Turquoise	No. 480 Gold
No. 460 Veil White	No. 461 Desert Tan	No. 462 Aquamarine	No. 463 Landon Green	No. 531 White	No. 532 Beige	No. 533 Cerulean Blue	No. 534 Vermilion
No. 464 Beige	No. 465 Flame	No. 466 Yellow	No. 490 Blue	No. 491 Brown	No. 494 Gold	No. 522 Sand Brown	No. 496 Coral
No. 500 Beige	No. 501 Autumn	No. 507 Beige	No. 508 Gold	No. 510 White	No. 511 Beige	No. 518 Wheat	No. 519 Fawn

SOFT FABRIC CHAIR COVERS

Available (with self welts) only on Chairs so specified in price list.

No. 482 Claret Red   No. 484 Gold

UNSUPPORTED VINYL PLASTIC CHAIR COVERS

Available only on "Plymouth House" Early American Chairs.

No. 487 Beige   No. 488 Gold   No. 489 Tangerine

Chair cover patterns, 1966.

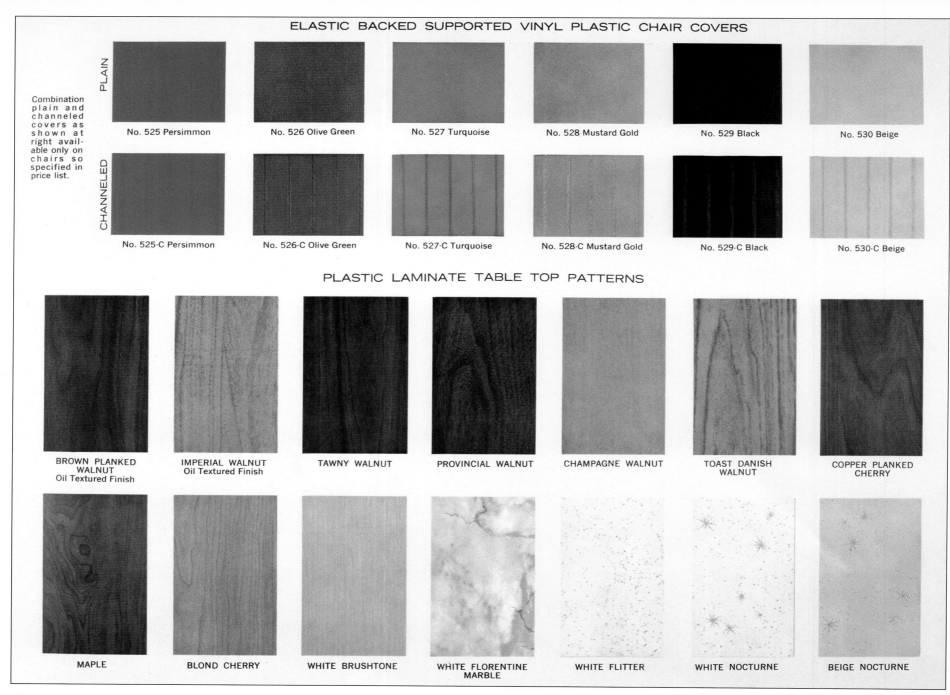

ELASTIC BACKED SUPPORTED VINYL PLASTIC CHAIR COVERS

PLAIN

Combination plain and channeled covers as shown at right available only on chairs so specified in price list.

No. 525 Persimmon

No. 526 Olive Green

No. 527 Turquoise

No. 528 Mustard Gold

No. 529 Black

No. 530 Beige

CHANNELED

No. 525-C Persimmon

No. 526-C Olive Green

No. 527-C Turquoise

No. 528-C Mustard Gold

No. 529-C Black

No. 530-C Beige

PLASTIC LAMINATE TABLE TOP PATTERNS

BROWN PLANKED WALNUT
Oil Textured Finish

IMPERIAL WALNUT
Oil Textured Finish

TAWNY WALNUT

PROVINCIAL WALNUT

CHAMPAGNE WALNUT

TOAST DANISH WALNUT

COPPER PLANKED CHERRY

MAPLE

BLOND CHERRY

WHITE BRUSHTONE

WHITE FLORENTINE MARBLE

WHITE FLITTER

WHITE NOCTURNE

BEIGE NOCTURNE

Chair cover and tabletop patterns, 1966.

92

ELASTIC BACKED SUPPORTED VINYL PLASTIC CHAIR COVERS

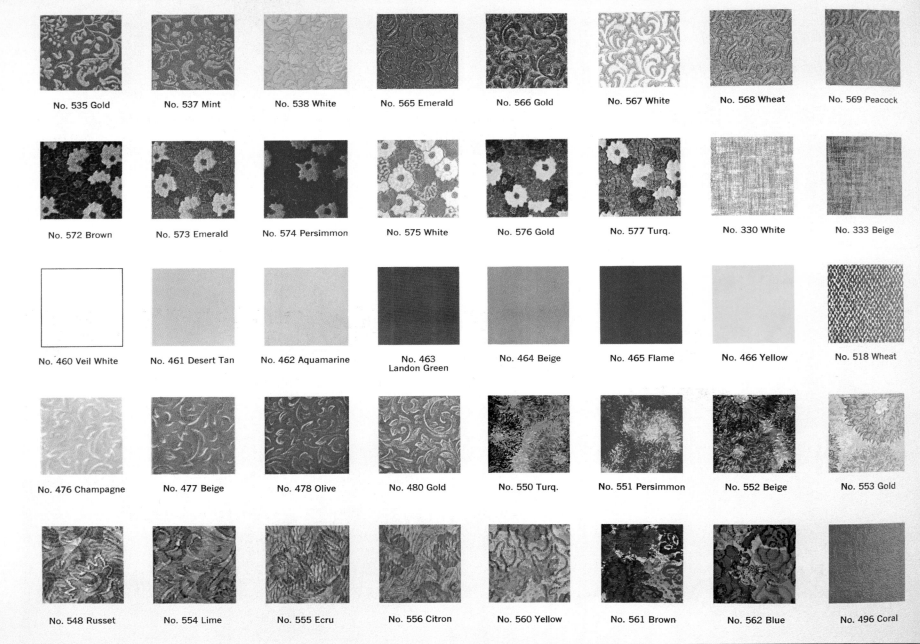

No. 535 Gold	No. 537 Mint	No. 538 White	No. 565 Emerald	No. 566 Gold	No. 567 White	No. 568 Wheat	No. 569 Peacock
No. 572 Brown	No. 573 Emerald	No. 574 Persimmon	No. 575 White	No. 576 Gold	No. 577 Turq.	No. 330 White	No. 333 Beige
No. 460 Veil White	No. 461 Desert Tan	No. 462 Aquamarine	No. 463 Landon Green	No. 464 Beige	No. 465 Flame	No. 466 Yellow	No. 518 Wheat
No. 476 Champagne	No. 477 Beige	No. 478 Olive	No. 480 Gold	No. 550 Turq.	No. 551 Persimmon	No. 552 Beige	No. 553 Gold
No. 548 Russet	No. 554 Lime	No. 555 Ecru	No. 556 Citron	No. 560 Yellow	No. 561 Brown	No. 562 Blue	No. 496 Coral

Chair cover patterns, 1967.

No. 557 Caramel

No. 558 Fern

No. 559 Nutmeg

No. 487 Beige

No. 488 Gold

No. 489 Tangerine

Nos. 487, 488 and 489 are UNSUPPORTED VINYL PLASTIC available only on "Plymouth House" Early American Chairs

No. 482 and No. 484 are SOFT FABRIC COVERS available only on chairs specified in Price List

No. 482 Claret

No. 484 Gold

No. 525-C Persimmon
No. 525 Persimmon — Plain

Combination Plain and Channeled covers as shown here, available only on chairs specified in Price List

No. 526-C Olive Green
No. 526 Olive Green — Plain

No. 528-C Mustard Gold
No. 528 Mustard Gold — Plain

No. 529-C Black
No. 529 Black — Plain

TAWNY WALNUT
Gloss Finish

BROWN PLANKED WALNUT
Textured Finish

IMPERIAL WALNUT
Textured Finish

GUNSTOCK WALNUT
Textured Finish

SILVER GRAY WALNUT
Textured Finish

FRUITWOOD
Satin Finish

SCANDIA TEAK
Textured Finish

MADRID OAK
Textured Finish

ROCK MAPLE
Textured Finish

WHITE BRUSHTONE
Satin Finish

WHITE FLORENTINE MARBLE
Gloss Finish

WHITE FLITTER
Gloss Finish

NOTE: Some laminates are not available on all tables — see Price List for availability

Chair cover and tabletop patterns, 1967.

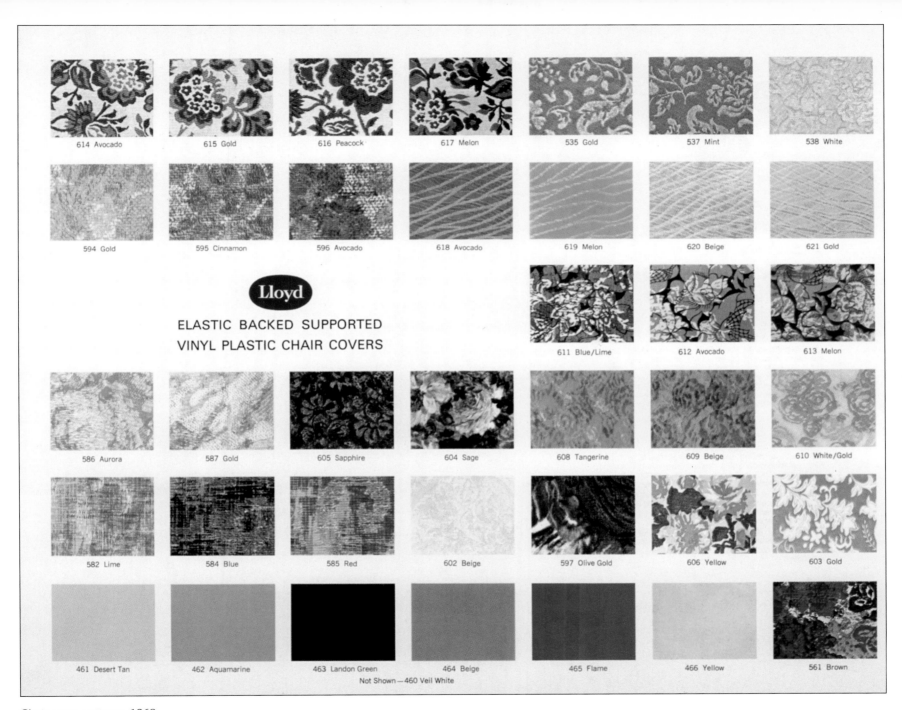

ELASTIC BACKED SUPPORTED
VINYL PLASTIC CHAIR COVERS

614 Avocado
615 Gold
616 Peacock
617 Melon
535 Gold
537 Mint
538 White

594 Gold
595 Cinnamon
596 Avocado
618 Avocado
619 Melon
620 Beige
621 Gold

611 Blue/Lime
612 Avocado
613 Melon

586 Aurora
587 Gold
605 Sapphire
604 Sage
608 Tangerine
609 Beige
610 White/Gold

582 Lime
584 Blue
585 Red
602 Beige
597 Olive Gold
606 Yellow
603 Gold

461 Desert Tan
462 Aquamarine
463 Landon Green
464 Beige
465 Flame
466 Yellow
561 Brown

Not Shown — 460 Veil White

Chair cover patterns, 1969.

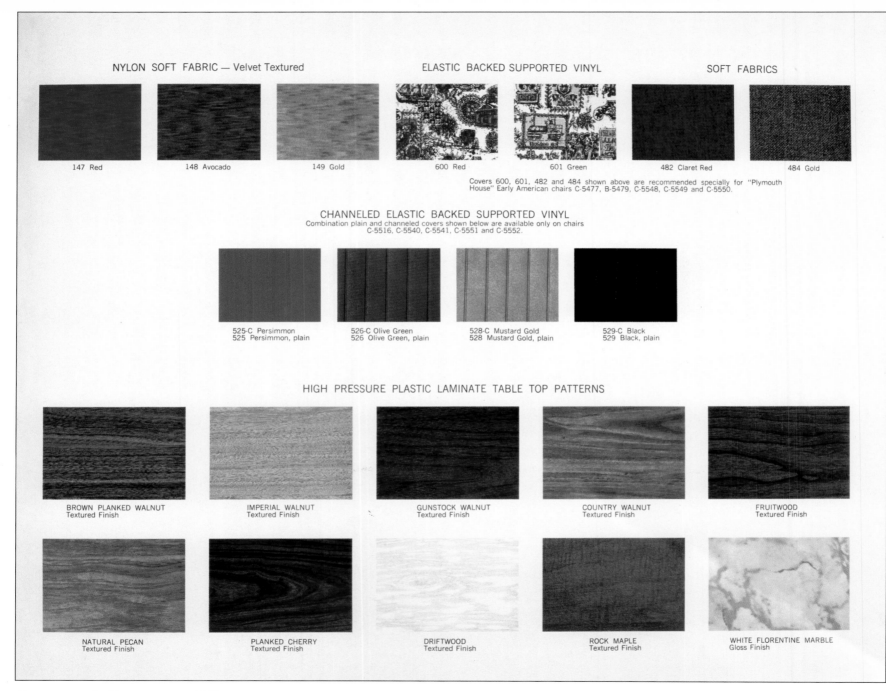

NYLON SOFT FABRIC — Velvet Textured

147 Red   148 Avocado   149 Gold

ELASTIC BACKED SUPPORTED VINYL

600 Red   601 Green

SOFT FABRICS

482 Claret Red   484 Gold

Covers 600, 601, 482 and 484 shown above are recommended specially for "Plymouth House" Early American chairs C-5477, B-5479, C-5548, C-5549 and C-5550.

CHANNELED ELASTIC BACKED SUPPORTED VINYL

Combination plain and channeled covers shown below are available only on chairs C-5516, C-5540, C-5541, C-5551 and C-5552.

525-C Persimmon
525 Persimmon, plain

526-C Olive Green
526 Olive Green, plain

528-C Mustard Gold
528 Mustard Gold, plain

529-C Black
529 Black, plain

HIGH PRESSURE PLASTIC LAMINATE TABLE TOP PATTERNS

BROWN PLANKED WALNUT
Textured Finish

IMPERIAL WALNUT
Textured Finish

GUNSTOCK WALNUT
Textured Finish

COUNTRY WALNUT
Textured Finish

FRUITWOOD
Textured Finish

NATURAL PECAN
Textured Finish

PLANKED CHERRY
Textured Finish

DRIFTWOOD
Textured Finish

ROCK MAPLE
Textured Finish

WHITE FLORENTINE MARBLE
Gloss Finish

Chair cover and tabletop patterns, 1969.

1970s Dinettes

Table T-8585 – Double Pedestal Base Extension Table, Chrome/Black Finish (1970) 36" x 48" x 72" surfboard shaped top includes two 12" leaves, as shown. 1 ½" plastic laminated self-edge. Chrome plated column with Black or Bronze stainless steel trimmed legs. Adjustable, self-aligning metal floor glides. Optional "bumper molding" protects the edges of table tops from accidental marring by swivel chairs. Also available in Chrome/Bronze finish.

Chair C-5568 – Pedestal Base Swivel Chair, Chrome/Black Finish (1970) Welted, circular shaped seat and back cushioned with urethane foam. Five-leg base offers greater stability—is virtually untippable. Nylon bushing affords smooth swivel action. Chrome plated pedestal column with Black or Bronze, stainless steel trimmed legs. Adjustable, self-aligning metal floor glides. Seat 17 ½" x 17 ½". Overall height 33 ¼". Also available in Chrome/ Bronze finish.

Set: $600-700

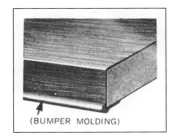

(BUMPER MOLDING)

Table T-8583 – Pedestal Base Extension Table, Chrome/Black Finish (1970)
42" diameter round top, extends to 42" x 60" oval, as shown, with 18" extension leaf. 1 ½" plastic laminated self-edge. Chrome plated pedestal column with Black or Bronze, stainless steel trimmed legs. Equipped with easy-acting ratchet extension top. Adjustable, self-aligning metal floor glides. Optional "bumper molding." Also available in Chrome/Bronze finish.

Chair C-5569 – Pedestal Base Swivel Chair, Chrome/Black Finish (1970)
Welted seat and high back cushioned with urethane foam. Five-leg base offers greater stability—is virtually untippable. Nylon bushing affords smooth swivel action. Chrome plated pedestal column with Black or Bronze, stainless steel trimmed legs. Adjustable, self-aligning metal floor glides. Seat 17 ½" x 17 ¼". Overall height 39 ¾". Also available in Chrome/Bronze finish.

Set: $650-750

Table T-8584 – Double Pedestal Base Extension Table, Chrome/Bronze Finish (1970)
38" x 48" x 60" surfboard shaped top, includes 12" extension leaf, as shown. 1 ½" plastic laminate self-edge. Chrome plated pedestal column with Bronze or Black stainless steel trimmed legs. Adjustable, self-aligning metal floor glides. Optional "bumper molding" protects the edges of table tops from accidental marring by swivel chairs. Also available in Chrome/Black finish.

Chair C-5570 – Pedestal Base Swivel Chair, Chrome/Bronze Finish (1970)
Welted, circular shaped seat and high back cushioned with urethane foam. Five-leg base offers greater stability— is virtually untippable. Nylon bushing affords smooth swivel action. Chrome plated pedestal column with Black or Bronze stainless steel trimmed legs. Adjustable, self-aligning metal floor glides. Seat 17 ½" x 17 ½". Overall height 39 ¾". Also available in Chrome/Black finish.

Set: $600-700

Table T-8583 – Pedestal Base Extension Table, Chrome/Bronze Finish (1970)
42" diameter round top, extends to 42" x 60" oval, as shown, with 18" extension leaf. 1 ½" plastic laminated self-edge. Chrome plated pedestal column with Black or Bronze stainless steel trimmed legs. Equipped with easy-acting ratchet extension top. Adjustable, self-aligning metal floor glides. Optional "bumper molding" protects the edges of table tops from accidental marring by swivel chairs. Also available in Chrome/Black finish.

Chair C-5567 – Pedestal Base Swivel Chair, Chrome/Bronze Finish (1970)
Welted seat and back cushioned with urethane foam. Five leg base offers greater stability—is virtually untippable. Nylon bushing affords smooth swivel action. Chrome plated pedestal column with Black or Bronze stainless steel trimmed legs. Adjustable, self-aligning metal floor glides. Seat 17 ½" x 17 ¼". Overall height 33 ¼". Also available in Chrome/Black finish.

Set: $500-600

Table T-8581 – Extension Table, Metallic Bronze Finish (1970)
42" x 48" oval top extends to 42" x 72" oval, as shown, with two 12" leaves. 1 ¾" plastic
laminated self-edge.

Chair C-5561 – Upholstered Back Chair, Metallic Bronze Finish (1970)
16" x 15 ½" seat and back cushioned with urethane foam. Early American decorative
motif on Maple finished wood back rail. Overall height 35".

Set: $500-600

Table T-8579 – Extension Table, Metallic Bronze Finish (1970)
36" x 48" oval top extends to 36" x 60" oval, as shown, with 12" leaf. 1 ¾" plastic laminated self-edge. Also available with two 12" leaves.

Chair C-5560 – Spindle Back, Metallic Bronze Finish (1970)
Seat 16" x 15 ½", cushioned with urethane foam. Tubular metal back spindles. Early American decorative motif on Maple finished wood back rail. Overall height 35".

Set: $350-450

Table T-8577 – Extension Table, Metallic Bronze Finish (1970)
42" diameter round top extends to 42" x 60" oval, as shown, with 18" leaf. 1 ¾" plastic laminate self-edge. Also available with two 15" leaves.

Chair C-5566 – "Fibercraft" High Back, Metallic Bronze Finish (1970)
Welted seat, 16 ½" x 16", cushioned with urethane foam. Exclusive Lloyd "Fibercraft" back panel with natural cane finish, as shown. Overall height 38".

Set: $550-650

Table T-8575 – Extension Table, Metallic Bronze Finish (1970) 36" x 48" x 72" rectangular top, including two 12" leaves, as shown. 1 ¾" plastic laminate self-edge.

Chair C-5565 – High Back, Metallic Bronze Finish (1970) Welted seat and upholstered back cushioned with urethane foam. Seat 16 ½" x 16". Overall height 38".

Set: $550-650

Table T-8574 – Extension Table, Metallic Bronze Finish (1970)
36" x 48" x 60" rectangular top, including 12" extension leaf, as shown. 1 ¾" plastic laminate self-edge.

Chair C-5564 – High Back, Metallic Bronze Finish (1970)
Welted seat, 16 ½" x 16", cushioned with urethane foam. Decorative back rest of solid welded rod.
Overall height 38".

Set: $450-550

Table T-8582 – Double Pedestal Base Extension Table, Goldtone Finish (1970)
42" x 60" x 84" rectangular shaped top, including two 12" extension leaves, as shown. 1 ¾" plastic laminate self-edge. Adjustable, self-aligning metal floor glides. Optional "bumper molding."

Chair C-5541 – Pedestal Base Swivel Chair, Goldtone Finish (1970)
Wide, contoured bucket seat cushion, 17 ½" x 16 ¾". Plastic laminated back rest in Brown Planked Walnut pattern only. Adjustable, self-aligning metal floor glides. Ball bearing swivel mechanism. Overall height 33".

Chair C-5516 – High Back, Goldtone Finish (1970)
Contoured, upholstered seat cushion, 17 ½" x 16 ¾". Plastic laminated back rest in Brown Planked Walnut pattern only. Overall height 34".

Set: $700-800

Table T-8487 – Goldtone Finish (1970) 36" x 48" x 60" top with 12" extension leaf in place, as shown. 1 ¾" thick plastic laminated self-edge. 1 ¾" diameter tapered legs with permanently knurled decoration. Leaf hanger for self storing of extension leaf. Also available with two 12" extension leaves.

Chair C-5563 – High Back, Goldtone Finish (1970) Welted seat and decorative oval shaped back cushioned with urethane foam. Seat 16 ½" x 16". Overall height 37".

Set: $450-550

Table T-8571 – Extension Table, Goldtone Finish (1970)
35" x 48" oval extends to 36" x 60" oval, as shown, with 12" leaf. 1 ¾" plastic laminate self-edge.

Chair C-5562 – High Back, Goldtone Finish (1970)
Welted seat and shaped back cushioned with urethane foam. Seat 16" x 15 ½". Overall height 36 ½".

Set: $400-500

Table T-8551 – Goldtone Finish (1970)
36" x 36" square top, as shown, extends to 36" x 60", with two 12" leaves. 1 ¾" plastic laminated self-edge. 1 ¾" diameter tapered legs, permanently knurled decoration.

Chair C-5516 – High Back, Goldtone Finish (1970)
Contoured, upholstered seat cushion 17 ½" x 16 ¾". Plastic laminated back rest in Brown Planked Walnut pattern only. Overall height 34".

Set: $350-450

Table T-8570 – Extension Table, Goldtone Finish (1970)
30" x 40" x 48" rectangular top, including 8" extension leaf, as shown. 1 ¾" plastic laminate self-edge.

Chair C-5502 – Goldtone Finish (1970)
Thickly upholstered, welted seat cushion, 16 ½" x 16". Elegantly designed gold colored metal back rest. Overall height 32 ¼".

Set: $350-450

Table T-8588 – Pedestal Base Extension Table, Bright Chrome Finish (1971)
42" diameter round top extends to 42" x 60" oval with 18" leaf in place, as shown. Top is
1 ¼" thick. Self-centering extension slides. Adjustable floor glides. Optional bumper molding.

Chair C-5575 – Bright Chrome Finish (1971)
18 ¾" x 16 ½" seat cushioned with urethane foam. Back panel of woven "Fibercraft,"
finished in Black only, as shown. Adjustable floor glides. Overall height 32".

Set: $800-1,000

Table T-8590 – Double Pedestal Base Extension Table, Bright Chrome Finish (1971)
36" x 48" x 72" top with two 12" leaves in place, as shown. Top 1 ¼" thick. Adjustable floor glides. Optional bumper molding. Also available with one 12" leaf.

Chair C-5576 – Pedestal Base Stationary Chair, Bright Chrome Finish (1971)
17" x 16 ¼" seat cushioned with urethane foam. Back of polyethylene in White, as shown, or Black. Adjustable floor glides. Overall height 33".

Set: $600-800

Table T-8591 –
Pedestal Base, Bright Chrome Finish (1971)
42" diameter round top. Top 1 ¼" thick. Adjustable floor glides. Optional bumper molding.

Chair C-5575 –
"Fibercraft" Chair, Bright Chrome Finish (1971)
18 ¾" x 16 ½" seat cushioned with urethane foam. Back panel of woven "Fibercraft," finished in Black only, as shown. Adjustable floor glides. Overall height 32".

Set: $800-1,000

Table T-8587 – Pedestal Base Game Table, Black Base (1971) 34" x 34" top, 1 ¼" thick. Available only with checkerboard design in Brown Planked Walnut or Country Walnut pattern. Adjustable floor glides. Optional bumper molding. Also available with white or bronze base.

Chair C-5574 – Pedestal Base Swivel Chair, Black Base (1971) 17" x 16 ¼" seat cushioned with urethane foam. Back of polyethylene in Black, as shown, or White. Adjustable floor glides. Height 33". Also available with white or bronze base.

Set: $600-800

Table T-8558-B – Pedestal Base Extension Table, Goldtone Finish (1971)
42" diameter round top extends to 42" x 60" oval with 18" leaf in place, as shown. Top 1 ¾"
thick. Self-centering extension slides. Adjustable floor glides. Optional bumper molding.

Chair C-5540 – Pedestal Base Swivel Chair, Goldtone Finish (1971)
17 ¾" x 17" seat cushioned with urethane foam. Back comfortably contoured and upholstered.
Ball bearing swivel mechanism. Overall height 36".

Set: $500-700

Table T-8572 – Extension Table, Goldtone Finish (1971)
36" diameter round top extends to 36" x 60" with two 12" leaves in place, as shown. Top 1 ¾" thick.

Chair C-5572 – "Fibercraft" Chair, Goldtone Finish (1971)
16" x 15 ½" seat cushioned with urethane foam. Woven "Fibercraft" back panel, natural cane finish only, as shown. Plastic laminated back rail in Country Walnut, as shown, or Brown Planked Walnut patterns, only. Overall height 34 ½".

Set: $300-400

Table T-8487 – Extension Table, Goldtone Finish (1971)
36" x 48" x 60" top with 12" leaf in place, as shown. Top 1 ¾" thick. Also available with
two 12" leaves.

Chair C-5573 – "Fibercraft" Chair, Goldtone Finish (1971)
16 ¼" x 16 ½" seat cushioned with urethane foam. Woven "Fibercraft" back panel,
natural cane finish only, as shown. Tapered legs. Overall height 36 ¼".

Set: $450-600

Table T-6304 – Pedestal Base, White Finish (1971) 30" diameter plastic laminate top with white vinyl bumper molding around edge. Top laminate in choice of White Florentine Marble or Driftwood and solid colors in Parrot Green, Gold, Yellow, or White. Adjustable floor glides.

Chair C-6303 – Swivel Chair, White Finish (1971) Upholstered seat and back cushioned with urethane foam. Smooth, effortless swivel action. Adjustable floor glides. 16" diameter round seat. Overall height 32 ½".

Set: $400-500

Table T-8647 – "Sawbuck Series," Bright Chrome Finish (1974)
36" x 54-72" rectangular shape top (one 18" leaf). Sawbuck style base has plastic laminate top and edges.
Removable center leaf stores in special compartment located under the table top. Equalizing extension gear
permits table top to be opened and closed by one person. Base remains stationary, only the top moves.

Chair C-5638 – "Sawbuck Series," Upholstered Back, Bright Chrome Finish (1974)
17 ½" x 16 ½" seat. Seat and back cushioned with urethane foam. Fully upholstered back. Overall height 35 ½".

Bench B-5639 – "Sawbuck Series," Bright Chrome Finish (1974)
16" x 45" seat, cushioned with urethane foam. Overall height 18".

Set (table and chairs): $500-600
Bench: 150-250

Table T-9114 – "Mediterranean Series," Double Pedestal Base, Satin Black Finish (1974) 42" x 42-60" octagon shape top (one 18" leaf). Plastic laminate top and edges. Center leaf extension. Base has adjustable glides.

Chair C-5612 – "Mediterranean Series," Upholstered Back, Satin Black Finish (1974) 17 ½" x 16 ½" seat. Seat and back cushioned with urethane foam. Fully upholstered back. Overall height 37 ½".

Set: $300-400

Table T-8602 – Drop Leaf, Goldtone Finish (1974)
36" x 25-60" surfboard shape top, pull-out extension legs. Plastic laminate top and edges. Full length piano hinges. Also available with one 12" leaf.

Chair C-5571 – Laminate/Grill Back, Goldtone Finish (1974)
16" x 17" seat, cushioned with urethane foam. Plastic laminate top rail in Brown Planked Walnut and Country Walnut patterns only. Overall height 34".

Set: $150-250

Table T-8649 –
Goldtone Finish (1974)
36" x 16-60" surfboard
shape top, pull-out
extension legs. Tapered
legs. Plastic laminate top
and edge. Full length
piano hinges.

Chair C-5640 – Cane
Back, Goldtone Finish
(1974)
16 ½" x 16" seat,
cushioned with urethane
foam. Walnut color
molded styrene back.
Overall height 34 ½".

Set: $150-200

Table T-8701 – Goldtone Finish (1974)
36" x 48-60" rectangular shape top (one 12" leaf). Tapered 1 ½" diameter legs with three debossed ring design. Plastic laminate top and edges. Center leaf extension.

Chair C-5642 – Upholstered Back, Goldtone Finish (1974)
16 ½" x 16" seat, cushioned with urethane foam. Fully padded and upholstered back panel. Overall height 36 ½".

Set: $200-350

Table T-8806 – Goldtone Finish (1974)
36" x 48-60" surfboard shape top (one 12" leaf). Tapered 1 ¾" diameter legs with four embossed, textured ring design. Plastic laminate top and edges. Center leaf extension.

Chair C-5643 – Upholstered High Back, Goldtone Finish (1974)
16 ½" x 16" seat, cushioned with urethane foam. Fully padded and upholstered back. Overall height 36 ½".

Set: $300-400

Table T-8912 – Double Pedestal Base, Goldtone Finish (1974)
42" x 42-60" round shape top (one 18" leaf). Adjustable glides. Plastic laminate top and edges with bumper molding. Center leaf extension.

Chair C-5598 – Upholstered Back, Pedestal Base Swivel Chair, Goldtone Finish (1974)
18" x 16" seat. Seat and back cushioned with urethane foam. Fully upholstered back. Overall height 32 ½".

Set: $400-500

125

Table T-9010 – Double Pedestal Base, Chrome Finish (1974)
42" x 48-60" oval shape top (one 12" leaf). Adjustable glides. Plastic laminate top and edges with bumper molding. Center leaf extension.

Chair C-5603 – Upholstered Back, Pedestal Base Swivel Chair, Chrome Finish (1974)
18" x 16" seat. Seat and back cushioned with urethane foam. Fully upholstered back. Overall height 32".

Set: $500-600

Table T-8623 – Single Pedestal Base, Chrome Finish, Glass Top (1974) 42" diameter round shape top. Adjustable glides. Non-extension smoked glass top.

Chair C-5605 – Molded Acrylic Back, Pedestal Base Swivel Chair, Chrome Finish (1974) 19" x 17" seat, cushioned with urethane foam. Smoke colored molded acrylic bucket. Overall height 32".

Set: $700-900

Table T-8658 – "Valencia,"
Bright Chrome Legs (1976)
Rectangular 36" x 54-72" top
(one 18" leaf). Spanish Oak
Parquet top.

Chair C-5653 – "Valencia,"
Bright Chrome Frame (1976)
#744 Tobacco seat and back,
both padded with urethane
foam.

Set: $650-750

Table T-8657 – "Sorrento," Bright Chrome Legs (1976)
Rectangular 36" x 48-60" top (one 12" leaf). Chef Block top.

Chair C-5654 – "Sorrento," Bright Chrome Frame (1976)
#F-7145 Brown seat and back, both padded with urethane foam. Button-tufted chair back.

Set: $500-600

Table T-8659 –
"Cortina," Bright Chrome Legs (1976)
Round 42" x 42-60" top (one 18" leaf). Imperial Block Maple top.

Chair C-5652 –
"Cortina," Bright Chrome Frame (1976)
Imperial Block Maple back panels, #746 Chestnut seat. Seat cushions padded with urethane foam.

Set: $350-450

Table T-8662 – "Canberra," Bright Chrome Base (1976)
Round 42" non-extension. Bronze Tableau top with clear plastic bumper molding.

Chair C-5653 – "Canberra," Bright Chrome Frame (1976)
#F-7146 Gold seat and back. Seat and back cushions padded with urethane foam.

Set: $500-600

Table T-8662 – "Manta," Bright Chrome Base (1976)
Round 42" non-extension, Chef Block top. Self-edge top
protected by clear plastic bumper molding. Adjustable glides

Chair C-5656 – "Manta," Bright Chrome Base (1976)
#752 White/#751 Lemon Peel seat and back. Urethane foam
padded seat unit.

Set: $550-650

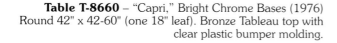

Table T-8660 – "Capri," Bright Chrome Bases (1976)
Round 42" x 42-60" (one 18" leaf). Bronze Tableau top with
clear plastic bumper molding.

Chair C-5658 – "Capri," Bright Chrome Base (1976)
#746 Chestnut seat and back. High back bucket-style swivel
seat unit padded in urethane foam.

Set: $400-500

Table T-8662 – "Montego," Bright Chrome Base (1976) Round 42" non-extension. Imperial Block Maple top with clear plastic bumper molding. Adjustable glides.

Chair C-5660 – "Montego," Bright Chrome Base (1976) Imperial Block Maple back only. #744 Tobacco seat. Urethane foam padded seat cushion.

Set: $350-450

Table T-8656 – "Hawaiian," Pineapple Legs (1976)
Round 42" x 42-60" (one 18" leaf). Autumn Oak top. Also available with Sweet Lime legs (see page 136).

Chair C-5650 – "Hawaiian," Pineapple Frame (1976)
Solid White back panels, #F-7142 Golden Rod seat. Urethane foam cushioned seat framed by colorful tubular steel. Also available with Sweet Lime frame (see page 136).

Set: $400-500

Table T-8652 – "Bostonian," Bright Chrome Legs (1976)
Rectangular 36" x 54-72" (one 18" leaf). Sylvan Oak top.

Chair C-5649 – "Bostonian," Bright Chrome Frame (1976)
Sylvan Oak back panels, #746 Chestnut seat. Urethane foam padded seats.

Set: $400-500

Table T-9201 – "Roma," Bright Chrome Legs (1976)
Rectangular 36" x 48-60" (one 12" leaf), Butcher Block top. Also available in Goldtone finish.

Chair C-5648 – "Roma," Bright Chrome Frame (1976)
Butcher Block back panels, #749 Chamois seat and back pillow. Also available in Goldtone finish.

Set: $350-450

Table T-8701 – "Bordeaux," Goldtone Legs (1976)
Rectangular 36" x 48-60" (one 12" leaf). Spanish Oak Parquet top. Debossed ring design on each table leg.

Chair C-5651 – "Bordeaux," Goldtone Frame (1976)
#756 Lemon seat and back. Fully upholstered cushions padded with urethane foam.

Set: $300-350

Table T-9201 – "Venetian," Bright Chrome Legs (1976)
Rectangular 36" x 48-60" (one 12" leaf), Solid White top. Also available in Goldtone finish.

Chair C-5647 – "Venetian," Bright Chrome Frame (1976)
Charcoal back panels, #F-7144 Martini seat. Urethane foam cushioned seats. Also available in Goldtone finish.

Set: $600-700

Table T-8656 – "Tahitian," Sweet Lime Legs (1976)
Round 42" x 42-60" (one 18" leaf), Celery Oak top. Also available with Pineapple legs (see page 134).

Chair C-5650 – "Tahitian," Sweet Lime Frame (1976)
Solid White back panels, #743 Clover seat. Urethane foam cushioned seats. Also available with Pineapple frame (see page 134).

Set: $400-500

Right:
Table T-8649 – Goldtone Finish (1976)
Surfboard shape 36" x 16-60", Country Walnut top. Tapered legs and self-edge top with full length piano hinges.

Chair C-5641 – Goldtone Finish (1976)
Country Walnut back, #765 Sunshine seat. Urethane foam padded seat.

Set: $150-250

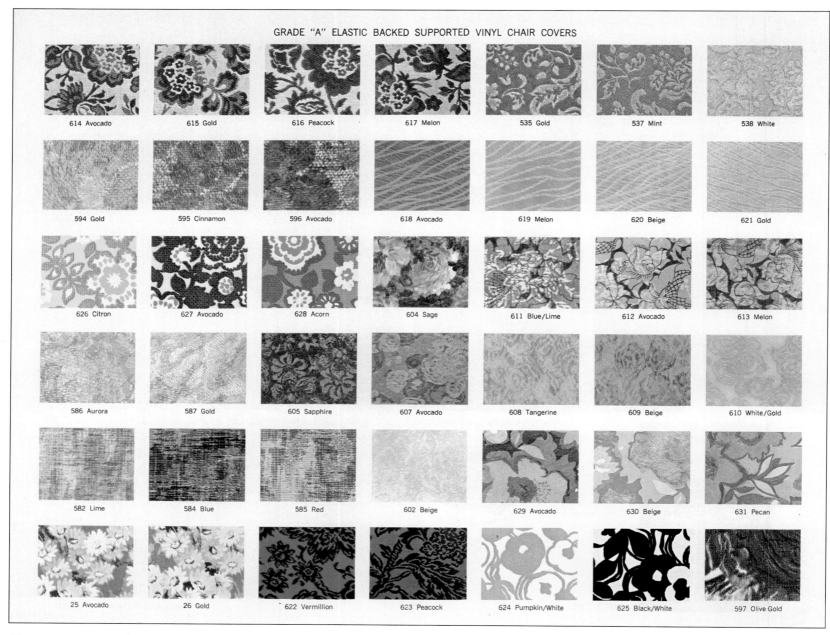

GRADE "A" ELASTIC BACKED SUPPORTED VINYL CHAIR COVERS

614 Avocado	615 Gold	616 Peacock	617 Melon	535 Gold	537 Mint	538 White
594 Gold	595 Cinnamon	596 Avocado	618 Avocado	619 Melon	620 Beige	621 Gold
626 Citron	627 Avocado	628 Acorn	604 Sage	611 Blue/Lime	612 Avocado	613 Melon
586 Aurora	587 Gold	605 Sapphire	607 Avocado	608 Tangerine	609 Beige	610 White/Gold
582 Lime	584 Blue	585 Red	602 Beige	629 Avocado	630 Beige	631 Pecan
25 Avocado	26 Gold	622 Vermillion	623 Peacock	624 Pumpkin/White	625 Black/White	597 Olive Gold

Chair cover patterns, 1970.

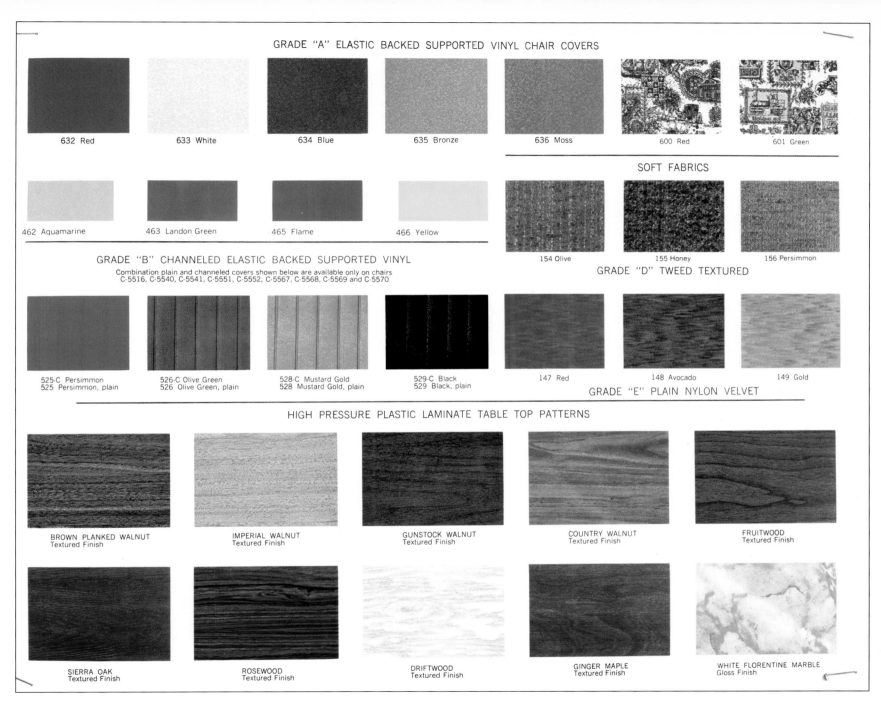

GRADE "A" ELASTIC BACKED SUPPORTED VINYL CHAIR COVERS

632 Red 633 White 634 Blue 635 Bronze 636 Moss 600 Red 601 Green

462 Aquamarine 463 Landon Green 465 Flame 466 Yellow

SOFT FABRICS

154 Olive 155 Honey 156 Persimmon

GRADE "B" CHANNELED ELASTIC BACKED SUPPORTED VINYL

Combination plain and channeled covers shown below are available only on chairs
C-5516, C-5540, C-5541, C-5551, C-5552, C-5567, C-5568, C-5569 and C-5570

GRADE "D" TWEED TEXTURED

525-C Persimmon
525 Persimmon, plain

526-C Olive Green
526 Olive Green, plain

528-C Mustard Gold
528 Mustard Gold, plain

529-C Black
529 Black, plain

147 Red 148 Avocado 149 Gold

GRADE "E" PLAIN NYLON VELVET

HIGH PRESSURE PLASTIC LAMINATE TABLE TOP PATTERNS

BROWN PLANKED WALNUT
Textured Finish

IMPERIAL WALNUT
Textured Finish

GUNSTOCK WALNUT
Textured Finish

COUNTRY WALNUT
Textured Finish

FRUITWOOD
Textured Finish

SIERRA OAK
Textured Finish

ROSEWOOD
Textured Finish

DRIFTWOOD
Textured Finish

GINGER MAPLE
Textured Finish

WHITE FLORENTINE MARBLE
Gloss Finish

Chair cover and tabletop patterns, 1970.

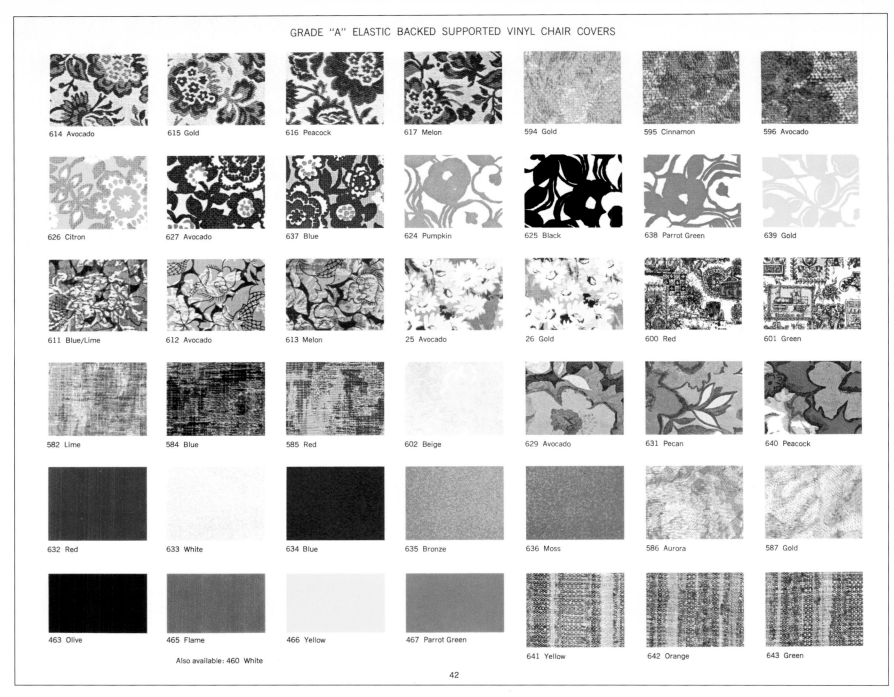

614 Avocado 615 Gold 616 Peacock 617 Melon 594 Gold 595 Cinnamon 596 Avocado

626 Citron 627 Avocado 637 Blue 624 Pumpkin 625 Black 638 Parrot Green 639 Gold

611 Blue/Lime 612 Avocado 613 Melon 25 Avocado 26 Gold 600 Red 601 Green

582 Lime 584 Blue 585 Red 602 Beige 629 Avocado 631 Pecan 640 Peacock

632 Red 633 White 634 Blue 635 Bronze 636 Moss 586 Aurora 587 Gold

463 Olive 465 Flame 466 Yellow 467 Parrot Green 641 Yellow 642 Orange 643 Green

Also available: 460 White

42

Chair cover patterns, 1971.

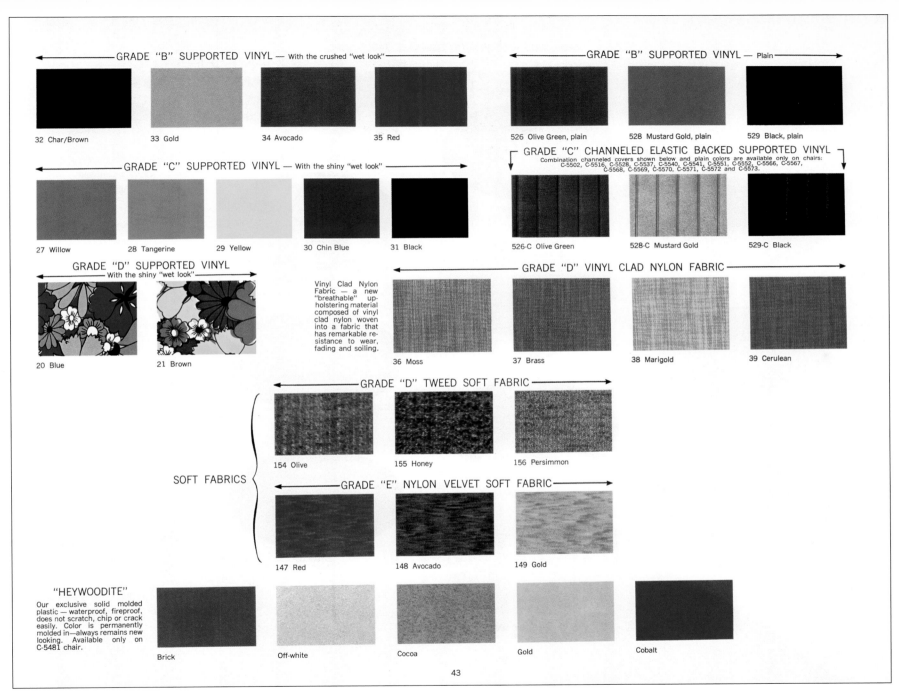

GRADE "B" SUPPORTED VINYL — With the crushed "wet look"

32 Char/Brown 33 Gold 34 Avocado 35 Red

GRADE "B" SUPPORTED VINYL — Plain

526 Olive Green, plain 528 Mustard Gold, plain 529 Black, plain

GRADE "C" SUPPORTED VINYL — With the shiny "wet look"

27 Willow 28 Tangerine 29 Yellow 30 Chin Blue 31 Black

GRADE "C" CHANNELED ELASTIC BACKED SUPPORTED VINYL
Combination channeled covers shown below and plain colors are available only on chairs: C-5502, C-5516, C-5528, C-5537, C-5540, C-5541, C-5551, C-5552, C-5566, C-5567, C-5568, C-5569, C-5570, C-5571, C-5572 and C-5573.

526-C Olive Green 528-C Mustard Gold 529-C Black

GRADE "D" SUPPORTED VINYL
With the shiny "wet look"

20 Blue 21 Brown

Vinyl Clad Nylon Fabric — a new "breathable" upholstering material composed of vinyl clad nylon woven into a fabric that has remarkable resistance to wear, fading and soiling.

GRADE "D" VINYL CLAD NYLON FABRIC

36 Moss 37 Brass 38 Marigold 39 Cerulean

SOFT FABRICS

GRADE "D" TWEED SOFT FABRIC

154 Olive 155 Honey 156 Persimmon

GRADE "E" NYLON VELVET SOFT FABRIC

147 Red 148 Avocado 149 Gold

"HEYWOODITE"
Our exclusive solid molded plastic — waterproof, fireproof, does not scratch, chip or crack easily. Color is permanently molded in—always remains new looking. Available only on C-5481 chair.

Brick Off-white Cocoa Gold Cobalt

43

Chair cover patterns, 1971.

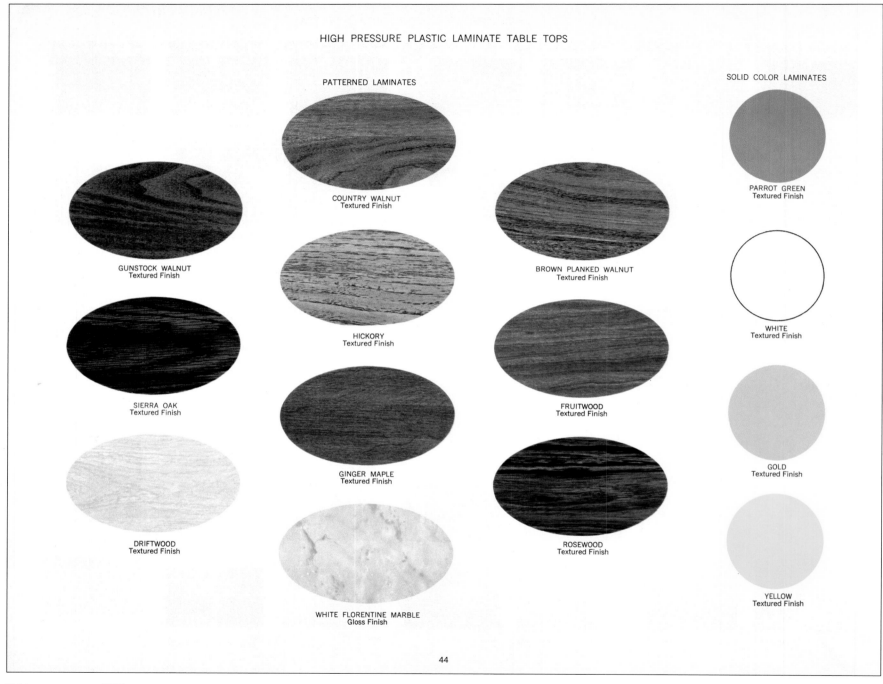

HIGH PRESSURE PLASTIC LAMINATE TABLE TOPS

PATTERNED LAMINATES

SOLID COLOR LAMINATES

PARROT GREEN
Textured Finish

COUNTRY WALNUT
Textured Finish

GUNSTOCK WALNUT
Textured Finish

BROWN PLANKED WALNUT
Textured Finish

WHITE
Textured Finish

HICKORY
Textured Finish

SIERRA OAK
Textured Finish

FRUITWOOD
Textured Finish

GOLD
Textured Finish

DRIFTWOOD
Textured Finish

GINGER MAPLE
Textured Finish

ROSEWOOD
Textured Finish

WHITE FLORENTINE MARBLE
Gloss Finish

YELLOW
Textured Finish

44

Tabletop patterns, 1971.

142

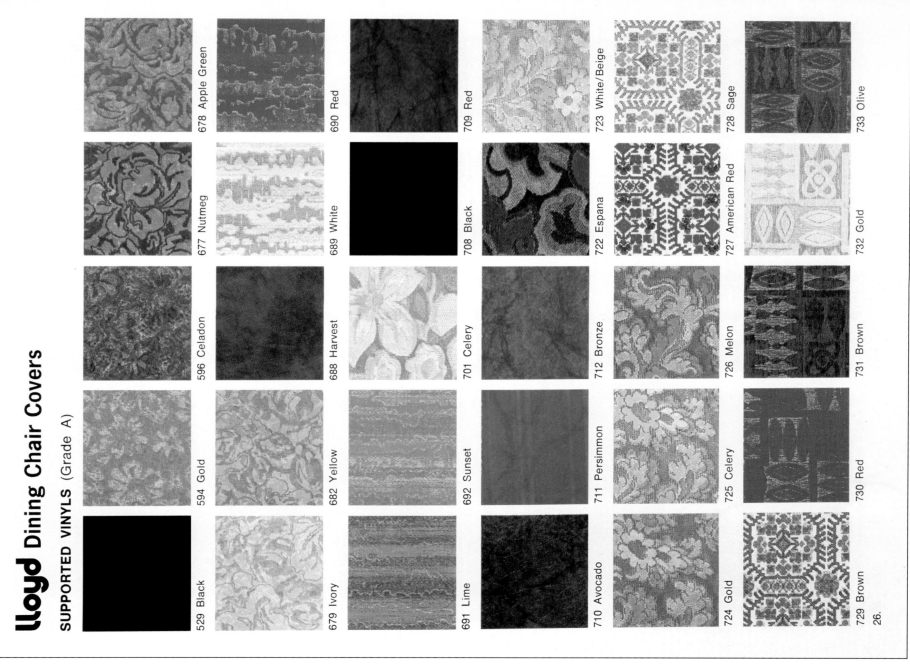

lloyd Dining Chair Covers

SUPPORTED VINYLS (Grade A)

678 Apple Green	690 Red	709 Red	723 White/Beige	728 Sage	733 Olive
677 Nutmeg	689 White	708 Black	722 Espana	727 American Red	732 Gold
596 Celadon	688 Harvest	701 Celery	712 Bronze	726 Melon	731 Brown
594 Gold	682 Yellow	692 Sunset	711 Persimmon	725 Celery	730 Red
529 Black	679 Ivory	691 Lime	710 Avocado	724 Gold	729 Brown

26.

Chair cover patterns, 1974.

143

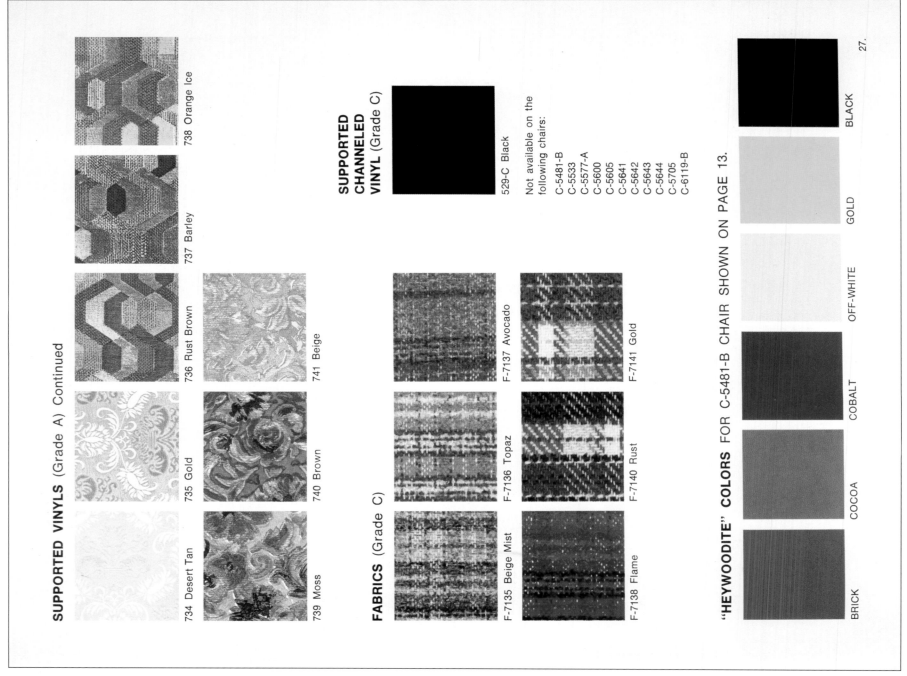

SUPPORTED VINYLS (Grade A) Continued

738 Orange Ice

737 Barley

736 Rust Brown

741 Beige

735 Gold

740 Brown

734 Desert Tan

739 Moss

SUPPORTED CHANNELED VINYL (Grade C)

529-C Black

Not available on the following chairs:

C-5481-B
C-5533
C-5577-A
C-5600
C-5605
C-5641
C-5642
C-5643
C-5644
C-5705
C-6119-B

FABRICS (Grade C)

F-7137 Avocado

F-7141 Gold

F-7136 Topaz

F-7140 Rust

F-7135 Beige Mist

F-7138 Flame

"HEYWOODITE" COLORS FOR C-5481-B CHAIR SHOWN ON PAGE 13.

BLACK

GOLD

OFF-WHITE

COBALT

COCOA

BRICK

27.

Chair cover patterns, 1974.

144

MEDICI OAK

CENTENNIAL PINE
Not available on T-8704, T-8705, T-8804 and T-8805 tables.

BUTCHER BLOCK
Not available on T-8704, T-8705, T-8804 and T-8805 tables.

IMPERIAL BLOCK MAPLE
Not available on T-8704, T-8705, T-8804 and T-8805 tables.

BUTCHER BLOCK INLAY
Available on T-8647 table only.

lloyd
**Dining Furniture
Plastic Laminate
Finishes**

BROWN PLANKED WALNUT

COUNTRY WALNUT

TAN KOLAWOOD

UNIVERSAL WALNUT

Tabletop patterns, 1974.

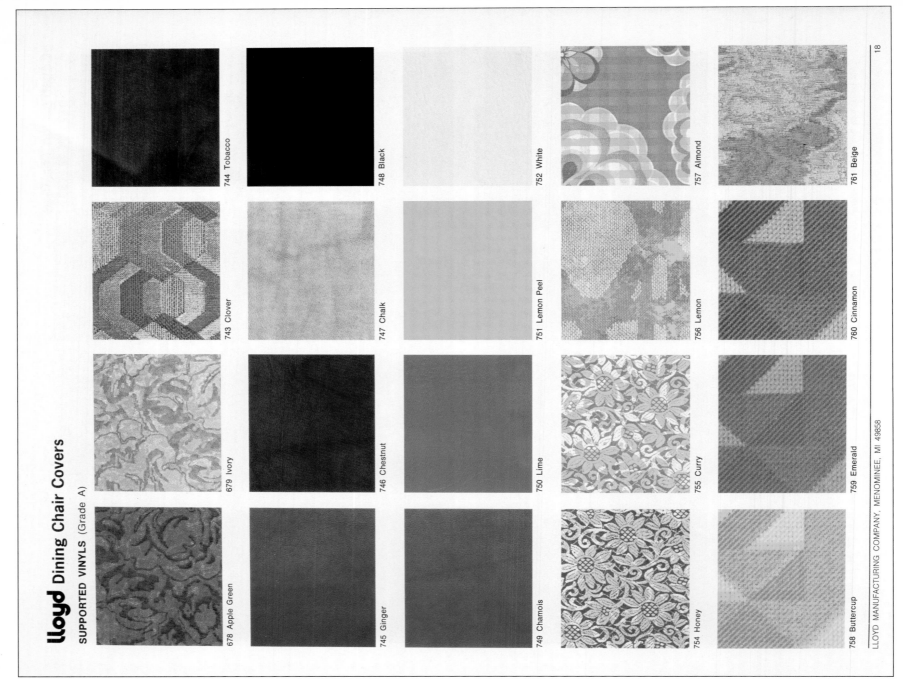

lloyd **Dining Chair Covers**
SUPPORTED VINYLS (Grade A)

678 Apple Green

679 Ivory

743 Clover

744 Tobacco

745 Ginger

746 Chestnut

747 Chalk

748 Black

749 Chamois

750 Lime

751 Lemon Peel

752 White

754 Honey

755 Curry

756 Lemon

757 Almond

758 Buttercup

759 Emerald

760 Cinnamon

761 Beige

LLOYD MANUFACTURING COMPANY, MENOMINEE, MI 49858

18

Chair cover patterns, 1976.

146

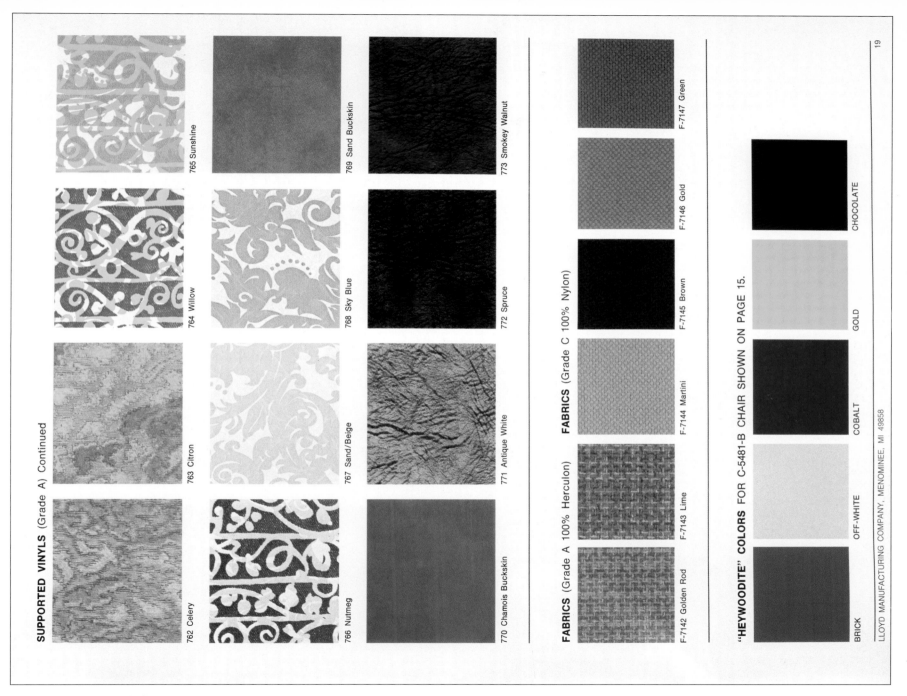

SUPPORTED VINYLS (Grade A) Continued

765 Sunshine

769 Sand Buckskin

773 Smokey Walnut

764 Willow

768 Sky Blue

772 Spruce

763 Citron

767 Sand/Beige

771 Antique White

762 Celery

766 Nutmeg

770 Chamois Buckskin

FABRICS (Grade C 100% Nylon)

F-7147 Green

F-7146 Gold

F-7145 Brown

F-7144 Martini

FABRICS (Grade A 100% Herculon)

F-7143 Lime

F-7142 Golden Rod

"HEYWOODITE" COLORS FOR C-5481-B CHAIR SHOWN ON PAGE 15.

CHOCOLATE

GOLD

COBALT

OFF-WHITE

BRICK

LLOYD MANUFACTURING COMPANY, MENOMINEE, MI 49858

19

Chair cover patterns, 1976.

147

Plastic Laminate Finishes

SYLVAN OAK

COUNTRY WALNUT

BROWN PLANKED WALNUT

UNIVERSAL WALNUT

IMPERIAL BLOCK MAPLE

BUTCHER BLOCK

BUTCHER BLOCK INLAY
Available on T-8647 table only.

SPANISH OAK PARQUE
Not available on T-8704, T-8705 tables.

BRONZE TABLEAU
Not available on T-8704, T-8705 tables.

AUTUMN OAK
Not available on T-8704, T-8705 tables.

CELERY OAK
Not available on T-8704, T-8705 tables.

CHEF BLOCK
Not available on T-8704, T-8705 tables.

LLOYD MANUFACTURING COMPANY, MENOMINEE, MI 49858

17

Tabletop patterns, 1976.

Wrought Iron and Cast Aluminum Dinettes

"Elegance" Dining Group
Table T-6078 (1963)
Chair C-6119 (1963)

Set: $500-600

"Natchez" Dining Group
Table T-6138 (1963)
Chair C-6139 (1963)

Set: $500-600

"Breezeway" Dining Group
Table T-6136 (1963)
Chair C-6137 (1963)

Set: $600-800

"Greenbrier" Dining Group
Table T-6151 (1964)
Bench B-6152 (1964)

Set: $600-700

"Olde Heritage" Dining Group
Table T-6184 – Pedestal Base, Semi-flat Black Finish (1966)
48" diameter round top with choice of White Florentine Marble or
Sierra Oak plastic laminated surface and self-edge. Tubular metal
base with ornamental scrollwork bracing, all hand welded. Black
plastic glides. Height 29".

Chair C-6185 – High Back, Semi-flat Black Finish (1966)
Thickly upholstered seat 16" x 17", with urethane foam cushioning.
Frame of solid round rod, hand welded. Black plastic glides.
Overall height 41 ¾".

Set: $400-500

"Magnolia" Dining Group (Cast Aluminum)
Table T-6092 (1964)
Chair C-6090 (1964)
S-6091 (1964)

Set: $450-550

"Castillian" Dining Group
Table T-6215 – Semi-flat Black Finish (1966)
A twist of the Mediterranean imparts distinctive flavor to this casual dining set. 42" round, solid plastic top.

Chair C-6219 – High Back, Semi-flat Black Finish (1966)
Thickly upholstered box type seat 16 ¼" x 17", with urethane foam cushioning. Frame of square, twisted rod, hand welded. Black plastic glides. Overall height 40 ½".

Set: $550-650

"New Orleans" Dining Group
Table T-6153 – Snow White or Avocado Finish (1966)
42" diameter round top with White Florentine Marble plastic laminate surface and self-edge. Legs of solid square rod, ornamented with metal leaf decoration, all hand welded. Plastic glides. Height 29".

Chair C-6155 – Snow White or Avocado Finish (1966)
Upholstered seat 17" x 15 ¾" with urethane foam cushioning. Frame of solid square rod with ornamental work to match table T-6153, all hand welded. Upholstered back rest cushion. Plastic glides. Overall height 32".

Set: $400-500

"Shasta Daisy" Dining Group
Table T-6214 (1966)
42" round, solid plastic top, somewhat
reminiscent of the old ice cream parlor.

Chair C-6216 – Snow White or Avocado
Finish (1966)
Upholstered seat 16" x 16 ¼" with urethane
foam cushioning. Frame of solid round rod, all
hand welded. Heart shaped upholstered back
rest. Plastic floor glides. Overall height 32 ½".

Set: $450-550

Table T-8557 – Ornamental Table, Black
Semi-Flat Enamel Finish (1967)
36" x 48" x 60" extension top including 12" leaf.
Self-edge plastic laminate top. Legs decorated
with wrought iron scrollwork and gold colored
metal ferrules.

Chair C-5539 – High Back, Black Semi-Flat
Enamel Finish (1967)
Scrollwork in back rest to match table. Black
extruded plastic welts. Gold colored metal
finials on back posts. Overall height 35 ½".

Set: $400-500

Table T-6260 – Pedestal Base, Semi-flat Black Finish (1969)
48" octagon shaped top, with Sierra Oak plastic laminated surface and self-edge. Mediterranean styled metalwork pedestal base, fitted with automatic self-leveling metal floor glides. Height 28 ¾".

Chair C-6262 – High Back, Semi-flat Black Finish (1969)
Thickly upholstered box type seat, 16 ¼" x 17", cushioned with urethane foam. Back rest has upholstered cushion with round rod scrollwork. Frame of solid square rod, hand welded. Glides are black plastic. Overall height 40".

Set: $450-550

Table T-6259 – Pedestal Base, Semi-flat Black Finish (1969)
48" diameter round top, with Sierra Oak plastic laminated surface and self-edge. Mediterranean styled metal work pedestal base, fitted with automatic self-leveling metal floor glides. Height 28 ¾". Also available with 42" diameter top.

Chair C-6261 – High Back, Semi-flat Black Finish (1969)
Thickly upholstered box type seat, 16 ¼" x 17", cushioned with urethane foam. Back rest of round rod scrollwork. Frame of solid square rod, hand-welded. Glides are black plastic. Overall height 40".

Set: $450-550

Table T-6121 – Snow White or Avocado Finish (1969)
42" diameter round top with White Florentine Marble plastic laminated surface and tapered edge banded with gold colored, anodized extruded aluminum. Legs of solid round rod, hand welded. Plastic floor glides. Height 29".

Chair C-6119 – Snow White or Avocado Finish (1969)
Upholstered seat 16" x 16 ½" cushioned with urethane foam. Upholstered back rest cushion on metal mesh. Hand welded solid round rod frame. Plastic floor glides. Overall height 34".

Set: $400-500

Table T-6121 – Snow White or Avocado Finish (1969)
42" diameter round top with White Florentine Marble plastic laminated surface and tapered edge banded with gold colored, anodized extruded aluminum. Legs of solid round rod, hand welded. Plastic floor glides. Height 29".

Chair C-6216 – Snow White or Avocado Finish (1969)
Upholstered seat 16" x 16 ¼" with urethane foam cushioning. Frame of solid round rod, all hand welded. Heart shaped upholstered back rest. Plastic floor glides. Overall height 32 ½".

Set: $400-500

Table T-6162 – Snow White or Avocado Finish (1969)
30" diameter round top with White Florentine Marble plastic laminated surface and tapered edge band with gold color, anodized extruded aluminum. Legs of solid round rod, hand welded. Plastic floor glides. Height 29".

Chair C-6119 – Snow White or Avocado Finish (1969)
Upholstered seat 16" x 16 ½" cushioned with urethane foam. Upholstered back rest cushion on metal mesh. Hand welded solid round rod frame. Plastic floor glides. Overall height 34".

Set: $300-350

Table T-6306 – Pedestal Base, White Finish (1971) 42" diameter plastic laminate top with white vinyl bumper molding around edge. Top laminate in choice of White Florentine Marble or Driftwood, and solid colors in Parrot Green, Gold, Yellow, or White. Adjustable floor glides.

Chair C-6292 – White Finish (1971) 17" x 16" upholstered seat cushioned with urethane foam. Decorative back of perforated white polyethylene in wrought iron frame. Non-marring plastic glides. Overall height 33".

Set: $500-650

Table T-6297 – White
Finish (1971)
42" diameter plastic laminate
top with white vinyl bumper
molding around edge. Top
laminate in choice of White
Florentine Marble or
Driftwood and solid colors in
Parrot Green, Gold, Yellow
or White. Cabriole styled legs
with non-marring plastic
glides.

Chair C-6291 – White
Finish (1971)
17" x 16" upholstered seat
cushioned with urethane
foam. Back of metal mesh.
Wrought iron frame. Non-
marring plastic glides. Overall
height 37".

Set: $450-550

Table T-6298 – Extension Table, White Finish (1971)
42" diameter top extends to 42" x 60" oval as shown, with leaf in place. Plastic laminate top with white vinyl bumper molding around edge. Laminate in choice of White Florentine Marble or Driftwood, and solid colors in Parrot Green, Gold, Yellow, or White. Cabriole styled wrought iron legs with non-marring plastic glides.

Chair C-6293 – White Finish (1971)
16" x 16 ½" seat cushioned with urethane foam. Wrought iron frame. Non-marring plastic glides. Overall height 33".

Set: $500-600

Table T-6300 – White Finish (1971)
42" diameter top with plastic laminate surface and self-edge. Laminate in choice of White Florentine Marble or Driftwood and solid colors in Parrot Green, Gold, Yellow, or White. Non-marring plastic glides. Also available with one 18" leaf.

Chair C-6299 – White Finish (1971)
17" x 15 ¾" seat and back cushioned with urethane foam. Square rod wrought iron frame. Non-marring plastic glides. Overall height 32".

Set: $450-550

Table T-6273 – Double Pedestal Base, Black Finish (1971)
42" x 48" oval top extends to 42" x 72" with two 12" extension leaves in place, as shown. Self-edge plastic laminate top surface in choice of Sierra Oak, as shown, Hickory, or White Florentine Marble. Adjustable metal floor glides. Optional "bumper molding." Height 28 ¾". Also available with one 12" leaf.

Chair C-6264-A – Black Finish (1971)
Seat 17" x 16". Wide, urethane foam cushioned seat and back. Black plastic snap-on glides. Overall height 38".

Set: $500-600

Table T-6269 – Pedestal Base, Black Finish (1971)
Top 42" x 42" non-extension, octagon shape, with self-edge plastic laminate surface in Sierra Oak, as shown, Hickory, or White Florentine Marble. Optional "bumper molding." Height 29".

Chair C-6265-A – Pedestal Base Swivel Chair, Black Finish (1971)
Seat 17" x 16". Wide, urethane foam cushioned seat and back. Overall height 38".

Set: $500-600

159

Bibliography

Greenwood, Richard N. *The Five Heywood Brothers (1826-1951). A Brief History of the Heywood-Wakefield Company during 125 Years.* New York: The Newcomen Society in North America, 1951.

Marshall Burns Lloyd Photo Gallery (http://mlloyd.org/gen/lloyd/mblphoto.htm)

Rouland, Steve and Roger. *Heywood-Wakefield Modern Furniture.* Paducah, KY: Collector Books, 1995.

Catalogs

Lloyd Trimline Dinettes, Chrome Dinettes, Wood Plastic-Top Dinettes (1954)

Metal Dinette Furniture, Lloyd (1961)
Dinette Furniture 1963
Lloyd Dinette Furniture 1964
Smart New Dinette Furniture by Lloyd (1965 – 1968 catalogs)
Smart Dinette Furniture by Lloyd for 1969
Dining Furniture for the 70s (c. 1970)
Dining Furniture, Lloyd of Menominee (1971)
Lloyd Creations in Metal Dining Furniture (1974)
Lloyd – Elegance in Dining Furniture (1976)